The Prehistoric Sites of Breconshire

GW00643612

Monuments in the Landscape

Volume IX

The Prehistoric Sites of Breconshire Ideology, Power and Monument Symbolism

by
George Children and George Nash

Logaston Press

LOGASTON PRESS
Little Logaston Woonton Almeley
Herefordshire HR3 6QH

First published by Logaston Press 2001
Copyright © George Children and George Nash 2001

ISBN 1 873827 57 1

Set in Times by Logaston Press
and printed in Great Britain by
Bell & Bain Ltd., Glasgow

For Betty and Betty

Acknowledgments

This book could not be possible without primary sources such as the Sites and Monuments Register (SMR) which is held at the Clwyd-Powys Archaeological Trust, as well as information from the National Monuments Register (NMR), Royal Commission for the Ancient and Historical Monuments of Wales (RCAHM[W]) and Cadw. Our sincere thanks goes to people within these organisations who provided invaluable information for this publication.

The authors would also like to thank the following people for their help with various components of this book. Sincere thanks goes to Frank Olding (until recently Curator of Abergavenny Museum), Bill Brittnell and Chris Martin of Clwyd-Powys Archaeological Trust (CPAT), and Peter Dorling of Brecon Beacons National Park (BBNP) who provided much material for publication including the wonderful aerial photographs of the Iron Age hill enclosures (CPAT), selective photographs of Bronze Age standing stones (BBNP) and illustrations from Brittnell and Savory's excellent *Gwernvale and Penyrwrlod: Two Neolithic Long Cairns in the Black Mountains of Breconshire*. Thanks are also due to Paul Jones for the various plans of the sites. Finally, a big thank you to Andy Johnson and Ron Shoesmith who took the time to harass, edit and produce this, our fourth book for this series.

George & George
September 2001

Contents

Please Note

Many of the monuments mentioned in this book are situated on private land and permission from the owner must, therefore, be obtained before visiting them.

The following points should also be observed:

1. When visiting sites in the countryside, always follow the Countryside Code.

2. On all sites, extreme care should be taken.

3. Any artefacts found on sites should be reported to the nearest museum or the Clwyd-Powys Archaeological Trust, 7a Church Street, Welshpool, Powys, SY21 7DL. Tel: 01938 553670.

4. Under no circumstances should visitors dig on or around any site. Any damage could result in prosecution.

5. It is an offence under the 1979 Ancient Monuments and Archaeological Areas Act to use metal detectors on or near scheduled ancient monuments. In addition, simple 'treasure hunting' near ancient monuments can damage evidence to such an extent that archaeologists are unable to interpret it fully in the future.

Preface

Four years and three county/regional volumes on, we have come to realise that change in prehistory, unlike change within our own time, is a process of only gradually emerging social complexity. This is very apparent in the material evidence. Walking through most regional museums the onlooker will start 'at the beginning'—the Palaeolithic—and progress through the various 'ages' to the miscellaneous bits and pieces of Victoriana. As he/she does so, a number of themes emerge, notably that tools or artefacts become more complex and intricate in design. The early Palaeolithic tools are mainly of one medium—flint. Towards the end of the Palaeolithic, bone and wood begin to appear in the archaeological record. As the visitor progresses further through time to the Iron Age, the same media are used, but in different ways. What unites all of the prehistoric displays is not so much the artefacts that are on view, as the ideas and emotions which are not.

The only artefacts that have usually survived the test of time from prehistoric days are inorganic items, such as stone tools and the odd fragment of pottery, although it is true that much can be gleaned from the organic remains of, say, a waterlogged site. Generally larger numbers of artefacts are found on a more recent site than on one of greater antiquity, but even so only a relatively small number can be crammed into a museum's glass case. This means that the museum visitor is inevitably presented with an unbalanced picture of the past. Based upon the evidence before them, they could be forgiven for believing that prehistoric society was minimalist in its operation. In this volume, as with the preceeding three, we have, in some ways controversially, hinted at the evidence of a non-material culture. We believe the key to understanding the monuments of Breconshire (Brycheiniog), or anywhere else, is their affinity with the landscape, and it is this theme which runs through much of the text. As the broader landscape is constructed within our minds, it results in landscape holding different meanings for different people. The Aboriginal perception of the Australian outback, for example, is vastly different from that of the white settler. Similarly, in prehistoric society, perceptions of landscape, and of the monuments constructed within it, would have been influenced by who you were and what strand of society you represented. Yet, how often are these considerations addressed by archaeologists? Productions such as Time Team and Meet the Ancestors make a valid attempt to reconstruct the past. Indeed, one occasionally hears the magic word 'symbolic', in reference to the non-functional aspects of material culture. What is sad, however, is that the day-to-day interpretations given by the county units deny social, political or symbolic factors any role at all. Artefacts and sites remain nothing more than just mere artefacts and sites.

As we have researched many different regions of Wales, we have found that a number of factors concerning monument sophistication reoccur. This would suggest that the task of producing a regional narrative such as this should become easier. However, the distribution of monuments and their place in the landscape potential and, therefore, their meaning are different. This regionality is best explored in a volume such as this.

In order to protect spots and sites where prehistoric artefacts have been found, we have only used eiyjer 4 or 6 figure grid refernces.

A note on Dating
For the dating used in this book, the following terms have been used:
>   bc (uncalibrated dates before Christ—those giving a
>   possible date range)
>   BC (Before Christ)
>   BP (Before Present, dates which are generally used for
>   environmental evidence relating to research carried out
>   before 1950 when radiocarbon dating was introduced.
These dates are derived from direct sources and are, in most cases, referenced as such.

The Stone Ages

Moulding a landscape:
The topography and geology of Breconshire

The geology of Breconshire and the surrounding counties has done much to shape the landscape. Topographically, the county is divided into three zones: mountain, plateau and valley. The mountain zone, located mainly in the south and west of the county, was formed by recent (Cenozoic) uplifting of the Black Mountains (rising to over 600m) and Brecon Beacons (rising to 700m) some 40 million years ago. The Black Mountains gently dip towards the south-south-east whilst the Brecon Beacons, oriented along a north-east/south-west alignment, rise steeply to the north and east. The plateau zone, located around the mountain zone, and regarded as part of the Breconshire uplands, is located within the central, eastern and northern parts of the county. It is believed that this zone was formed by either sub-aerial erosion or by weathering of ancient marine platforms. Although valleys occur throughout the county, the main areas where valley 'strikes' (a large directional horizontal line along and through a rock stratum creating a contoured land surface) occur are the Usk-Llynfi Basin (between Hay-on-Wye and Crickhowell) and the Builth-Llanwrtyd Depression (RCAHM[W] 1997:1; Pringle & Neville 1970:94-5).

Most of Breconshire consists of Old Red Sandstone (made up of fine marls, mudstones, siltstones and occasional sandstone conglomerates) which was formed some 370 million years ago during the Devonian period when much of the area was covered by a warm 'brackish' sea—very little fossil evidence comes from the these rocks. Around the Black Mountains the sandstones are up to

950m thick (*ibid.*:53). To the south of the county and running along the border with Monmouthshire, an extensive limestone and mill-stone grit outcropping occurs dating to the Carboniferous period (between 280 and 345 million years ago).

In the north-western part of the county are the Ludlow, Wenlock and the more extensive Llandovery series of sedimentary sandstone conglomerates, grits, mudstones, shales and silty flags. These date to the Silurian period (between 395 and 435 million years ago).

As part of the geomorphological story of the county, the final shaping of the landscape caused by the last ice age (referred to as the Late Devensian Glaciation) can not be ignored. The rapid retreat of the Welsh Ice Cap left large accumulations of till (boulder clay deposits) and re-shaped the valley profiles and created numerous fluvio-glacial landforms (such as eskers, kames, melt-water channels, moraines and ice-dammed lakes). Llangorse Lake and the classic 'U'-shaped Cwm Sorgwm Valley, near Talgarth are products of the glacial retreat which occurred around 14,500 years ago. It was shortly after this that humans arrived in the landscape— the first Breconshire hunter/gatherers.

Palaeolithic and Mesolithic Presence in Breconshire
A journey into the remote prehistory of this Welsh border county takes us back to an alien and inhospitable world devoid of all familiar man-made landmarks—villages, castle ruins, church spires rising above rolling fields, and tree-covered Iron Age hill enclo-sures (also referred to as hillforts). As the journey progresses, the traces of human activity become ever more slight. The enigmatic standing stones—a legacy of early Bronze Age society, and the tombs of the Neolithic—the visible remains of an early farming community's belief in the afterlife, all vanish as the landscape regresses from open field to dense wildwood. Beyond this point there are no substantial remains at all, no earth and stone heaped up to create a home or lasting memorial, no obvious signs that human beings ever inhabited this part of the world. All that remains of societies that were undoubtedly complex in structure and rich in mythology, are a few scattered implements fashioned by hunters skilled in the art of working flint and stone. As the journey continues, the climate deteriorates sharply, until the landscape can

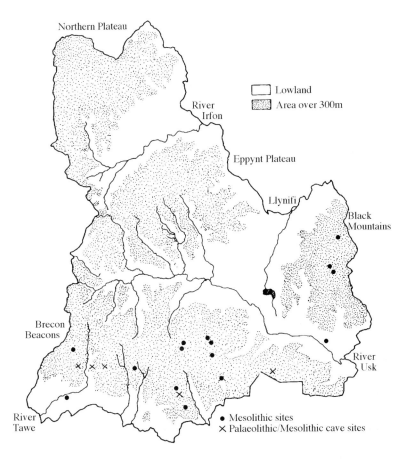

Distribution Map of Palaeolithic and Mesolithic Sites

no longer support dense broadleaf woods abundant in wildlife. Species that thrive on warmth seek refuge farther south. Red deer, wild cattle and pig—creatures of the forest—are not yet present in the northerly latitudes. Only elk, horse, reindeer and other cold-adapted species are robust enough to endure the freezing temperatures. Conditions worsen and the landscape is now a treeless desert. Most of Britain and all of Northern Europe lie entombed in ice. Up to 1km thick, glaciers covered all of Wales, sculpting the dramatic east-facing ridge of the Black Mountains as they crept south. Most of the west and north Midlands was swallowed up, as well as the

3

Wash and North Sea. The ice margin cut Herefordshire and Monmouthshire from north to south. Remains of extinct ice age animals discovered at King Arthur's Cave, overlooking the River Wye between Ross-on-Wye and Monmouth, indicate just how extreme an environment the Welsh border area then was: a hostile polar desert similar to present-day southern Greenland, populated by woolly rhinoceros, horse, giant deer, wild ox, hyena and mammoth.

The severity of the climate profoundly affected settlement and it was long believed that, at the height of the last ice age (c.25,000 BC), conditions in Southern Britain were far too cold for humans. Recent radiocarbon dating on human bone from Paviland Cave, on the Gower coast, however, has shown this was not the case and that people visited the cave around 26,550 bc (this new date replaces an old radiocarbon date of 16,510 bc). We can only speculate as to their reasons for wishing to do so, but the remains of a human body (the so-called 'Red Lady of Paviland', who was actually a male) carefully interred within the cave and sprinkled with red ochre, perhaps symbolising re-birth, indicate that these people shared with us a concern for death and the afterlife. By 20,000 BC, a massive expanse of ice covered the whole of Wales, referred to as the Welsh Ice Cap (Lowe and Walker 1984). No other contemporary human remains have been recovered in this part of Britain.

With regards to prehistoric occupation of caves within the limestone area of Breconshire, nothing is recorded before the Late Bronze Age (around 1000 BC). The Dan yr Ogof cave, excavated between 1938 and 1950 and one of Wales' most complex cave systems, did reveal prehistoric artefacts. These, however, dated to the Beaker period (c.2500 BC) including a gold bead, rapier, bronze razor and a small collection of Bronze Age flints.

Elsewhere in Paleolithic Europe a revolution was underway. The Upper Palaeolithic (35,000-10,000 BC) witnessed an explosion in human creativity, most spectacularly evident in the cave art of south-western France and northern Spain (the Dordogne, Lot and Pyrenees regions). This depicts naturalistic scenes involving large mammals such as mammoth, horse and reindeer. The art of this period was probably not art as we understand the concept today; painting was probably an act full of symbolic meaning which contained messages that could be 'read' by certain people. Careful inspection of the cave-wall frescoes shows that many of the animals painted were being hunted with bow and arrow. At the famous sites of Lascaux, a number of animals, including a wild horse, have arrows embedded in the torso. The art is sometimes regarded today as a form of hunting magic, possibly symbolising what had been hunted or what was to be hunted. There are obviously many other ideas concerning the origin and meaning of prehistoric art, far too numerous to cover in this volume, but the rock art of France and Spain does give an insight into the minds and capabilities of people who hunted along the ice margins of Wales. More importantly, some of the faunal remains found in Britain that date to the Upper Palaeolithic are also present on the cave walls of the Dordogne suggesting that similar hunting regimes were being practiced. The art of France and Spain dates from around 18,000 BC and was being executed at a time when summer temperatures were rising and the northern European and North American ice sheets, in particular the Fennoscandian and Lauentide, were in retreat. So far, in Britain, no rock art has been discovered. It is probable that due to the harsher conditions in Britain, certainly up until about 12,000 BC, no hunter/gatherer groups became fully established and art would not have been of the same importance to people using caves only on a temporary basis.

Before the emergence of so-called 'high art', Europe belonged to the Neanderthals, whose capacity for innovation appears to have been limited. With the appearance of anatomically modern humans (*homo sapiens sapiens*) from about 40,000 years ago, stagnation gave way to rapid social, technological and economic progress. A much wider range of tools came into use, indicating a greater willingness to work organic materials such as bone and antler. Greater dexterity was made possible by refinements such as bone needles which enabled more elaborate clothing to be made. Organic material such as bone, leather, wood, although undoubtedly widely used at this time, have long since perished unless preserved in the calcareous deposits of a cave or rock shelter. This is why the archaeological record is dominated by flint and stone tools, which, by themselves, say little and need to be amplified by reference to accounts drawn from contemporary or historically recorded hunter/ gatherer communities. Settlements became much more dense and there is evidence for the emergence of the first ethnic groups, defined partly by different styles of artefacts. Trading or exchange networks spanning hundreds of kilometres involved the movement of high-quality flint and in some cases, sea shells. Hunting became much more specialised, often focusing upon a single species. Unlike the opportunistic approach of earlier predators, Upper Palaeolithic peoples displayed a much higher degree of planning, co-ordination and awareness of herd movements. Communication between neighbouring groups would have enabled the close monitoring of favoured species, such as reindeer and wild horse. Social networks would also have provided insurance against local food shortages, especially around the ice margins, where the availability of food would have been particularly unpredictable.

From about 18,000 BC, a gradual thaw began to transform the Welsh landscape. After 16,000 BC, the ice sheets retreated ever more rapidly and over the next 4,000 years, sub-Arctic tundra plants, including sedges, grasses, mosses, lichens and dwarf birch and willow, colonised southern Britain. This rich mosaic of plant life in turn attracted migratory animals such as elk, horse and reindeer, pursued by small groups of hunters, who may well have used caves along the lower Usk Valley, above Crickhowell, as temporary summer bases. Winters around 10,000 BC remained cold, with average temperatures as low as -5 degrees centigrade (Lowe & Walker 1984). Only a handful of Late Upper Paleolithic sites are known in this part of Wales, many amounting to nothing more than scatters of flint and stone. Traces of human activity have been found in disturbed river gravels or close to later Neolithic monuments, but nothing yet in the carboniferous limestone caves above Garn Coch on the southern side of the Usk has been found. Much of the existing evidence is concentrated in the lower Usk Valley where finds consist mainly of flint waste (or debitage). It is probable that this flint may have been lost during hunting expeditions, and care must be taken in interpreting these finds. Furthermore, the effects of periglacial activity (permafrost, solifluction, riverine activity and moraine deposition) may have also confused the picture by re-arranging or completely destroying parts of the archaeological record. However, one site where there was substantial Palaeolithic activity is the Neolithic chambered tomb of

Gwernvale, 1.5km north of Crickhowell. During the excavation of this site, Palaeolithic and Mesolithic flint were found beneath the southern section of the façade, suggesting that this site was in use (albeit periodically) for up to 7,000 years prior to the construction of the Neolithic monument (Britnell & Savory 1984). This site may represent only a fraction of the total number of open sites (as distinct from caves) that once existed in the lower Usk Valley (see below).

Gwernvale: a Late Upper Palaeolithic hunting station
The tool kit needed to hunt, kill and butcher large migratory animals such as reindeer and horse established the specialist hunter throughout north-west Europe. Small hunting parties set up short-term camps along migration trails (Grønmow 1987), such as the well-known 'mass-kill' sites of Meiendorf and Stellmoor, in northern Germany. At Stellmoor A, there is evidence of reindeer-skinning, butchering, filleting, marrow-fracturing and the crushing and boiling of bones. Similar strategies, based on the seasonal movement of herds and humans, are well documented elsewhere (*e.g.* Cantabrian Spain). At broadly the same time, hunters were active in the area around Gwernvale. Regarded as the earliest open site in Wales (dating to around 10,000 BC), Late Upper Palaeolithic Gwernvale probably served as a base camp for the hunting of large migratory animals, such as reindeer and horse (Campbell 1977:107-8). Atop a raised plateau, the site would have been an ideal vantage point from which to monitor herds as they moved north/south through the steep-sided valley of the lower Usk, alternating between summer and winter grazing (*ibid.* 1977:114).

The majority of Late Upper Palaeolithic flint discovered at Gwernvale was found within an ancient buried soil (or palaeosol) and comprised an array of chalcedonic chert and backed blades (Healey & Green 1984:130). Tools included a 'penknife' point, blades, a microlith and microburin. Also present were classic Mesolithic tools including 56 microliths (23 of these were broad-backed, dating to the Early Mesolithic), 10 microburins, 5 notched blades and 10 truncated blades. The flint used to manufacture these tools was imported, possibly from the south-west Wales coast, and was either acquired directly from source or traded between inland

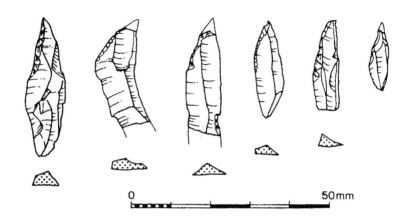

Mesolithic flint tools (microliths) from underneath the Gwernvale monument (from Britnell and Savory 1984)

hunting groups and coastal settlers, an arrangement that may be a form of gift exchange (see Barker 1992). It has been argued (Bender 1978) that such exchange alliances played a key role in establishing permanent settlement, that is, settlement within a defined territory. This idea is based on a system that operated among the American Indians of the Pacific north-west coast, where, it is suggested, alliances were created through the exchange of prestige goods. In order for transactions to take place, each group needs a stable means of production. The rich seasonal food resources available during the Late Upper Palaeolithic, coupled with a fragmentary settlement pattern of coastal and inland sites, make this model an interesting option to consider.

Intensive carcass utilisation is apparent throughout Europe during the succeeding Mesolithic period, when hunters concentrated on red deer, and, in coastal areas, large marine mammals such as killer whale and porpoise (Smith 1992). Nothing, it would seem, was left to waste. Unfortunately, the acidic soils in this part of Wales have destroyed all trace of such activities. The lithic evidence leaves the question open. Whereas generally, the tool kit of the Mesolithic hunter/gatherer appears to be more refined and specialised than that of his Late Upper Palaeolithic counterpart, reflecting a need to hunt, kill and butcher new kinds of animals, many of the tool types found at Gwernvale appear to have remained in use for very long periods. It is likely that Gwernvale, even during the Mesolithic, remained a temporary encampment used for the exploitation of cloven-hoofed animals (Jacobi 1980:183).

The proliferation of such sites during the Mesolithic, when hunting groups may have ranged in size from 45 to 240 people (Rowly-Conwy 1981), implies considerable social complexity. There have been many attempts to suggest some form of political/economic territorial structure for the Mesolithic and this has been argued with vigour concerning groups in southern Scandinavia (Nash 1998). Although some would disagree (Healey and Green 1984:129), contemporary hunter/gatherer evidence, in particular Inuit and Lapp settlement, does suggest that Mesolithic hunter/gatherers may have had some loosely-defined territorial structure, with prime hunter/gatherer land restricted to the fertile, tundra-steppe valleys of south Wales. Each of these territories would have depended for its viability on a number of variables, including the abundance and diversity of resources coupled with seasons of shortages of certain produce; migratory patterns of wildlife; settlement distribution; the state of technological development; willingness to co-operate in hunting and food gathering as opposed to competition for resources with neighbouring groups; per capita productivity and population density (Yesner 1980). During this period especially towards the Late Mesolithic, there is a definite shift from a semi-nomadic economy to semi-permanent or even permanent settlement. This may go some way to explain why large quantities of imported Mesolithic flints are present around the Gwernvale monument and elsewhere around the Black Mountains massif.

The 'climatic optimum' and the emergence of advanced hunter/gatherers

The lengthy transition from the Late Upper Palaeolithic to the Early Mesolithic is mainly characterised by minute changes in the size and shape of tiny blades, or microliths, over at least 2,000 years. These developments suggest gradual changes in hunting and gathering strategies, as broad-leaved woodland (also known as 'wildwood' or 'climax' woodland) began to colonise this area from the south. With the gradual northerly movement of the broad-leaved wildwoods new forest dwellers began to emerge such as roe deer and wild pig. A few notable indications of pre-Neolithic activity in the southern part of the county include quantities of datable charcoal and tree pollen, suggesting the encroachment of early Holocene (post-glacial) forests (RCAHM[W] 1997) and possible pre-Neolithic slash-and-burn woodland clearance strategies (as evidenced by datable charcoal found at Nant Heln and Coed Taf). Apart form a short and very severe 'blip' between 11,000 and 10,000 BC (the Loch Lomond stadial or cold phase), the climate gradually warmed throughout the transitional period. By 10,000 BC, birch, willow, juniper and, in some areas, pine, had migrated northwards. These species were subsequently replaced by elm, lime and alder (Huntley 1990). Eventually, from the onset of the Mesolithic, oak, hazel and elm began to flourish as the so-called 'climatic optimum' set in around 8000 BC; afterwards average summer temperatures were a degree or two higher than today. Ash and lime had also started to colonise the Breconshire woodlands which, by 6000 BC, had encroached up to altitudes of 450m. As sea levels rose, Britain, previously part of mainland Europe, became an island separated from the Continent by the newly-formed English Channel and North Sea.

Only around 18 Mesolithic sites or findspots have been recorded in Breconshire with a further 16 in neighbouring Radnorshire (RCAHM[W] 1997:17; Wymer 1977). Occasionally, these sites contain Mesolithic flint overlaid by later material. More often, however, they occur as scatters (varying quantities of flint found on an ancient surface). Radiocarbon dates have been established for only three of these Mesolithic sites, the earliest being 7200 BC at Waun Fignen Felen. Nearly all Mesolithic activity is confined to the foothills and hinterlands of the Black Mountains and the limestone plateaus within the south of the county. Around a large boggy peat basin on Waun Fignen Felen, two excavations revealed up to 70 pieces of unstratified flint including microliths, a scraper and notched blade. One of the excavations revealed a possible settlement floor consisting of a sand mound, a small pit and a hole which held a single stone, such as a hearth stone (RCAHM[W] 1997:19). More lithics and a perforated shale disc have been discovered in test pits close to a lake at the site, indicating that this area was more than just a place to hunt. Earliest dates for human activity around this area are set to 8000 BC. It is suggested that, apart from lithics, human activity included the removal of vegetation through burning. This activity lasted for 2,000 years resulting in an imbalance within the local ecology creating acid soils and the formation of blanket peat. Other flint scatter sites include Cantref (SN 986 188), Llanfihangel Abergwesyn (SN 85 52), Penderyn (SN 994 098), and Ystradfellte (SN 925 157).

Hunter/gatherers probably moved into the area from the south, via the lower Severn and Avon (Worcestershire) valleys, or west, along the upper reaches of the Wye and Usk. These early settlers may have attributed mythical significance to the imposing mountains, just as the complex 'creation' or 'dreamtime' myths of the Australian Aborigines refer to certain spiritually powerful features in the landscape of the Northern Territories, incorporating hills, lakes and watering holes, rocks possessing human characteristics and various animals. The discovery that some later burial monuments overlie Mesolithic scatters suggests that sites retained their sacred significance over many generations. Although products of a new socio-political order, that of the Neolithic, the monuments appear to be directly influenced, both in terms of form and orientation, by traditional ideas and beliefs associated with the local landscape. Rather than following a consistent orientation, east/west, for example, monuments are aligned to various local topographic features, such as mountain spurs, escarpments, natural cairns, rock outcrops, streams, springs and river valleys, and exhibit a diverse and complex structure. Likewise, Mesolithic activity around the east of the county is oriented towards the visual and symbolic draw of the Black Mountains. The extensive lithic scatters found in neighbouring Herefordshire and Radnorshire as well as Breconshire appear to be sited on the intermediate slopes and upper sections of the valley floor that face the Black Mountains (see Children and Nash 1994).

A Spreading Material Culture: The Neolithic of Breconshire
With the Neolithic (or New Stone Age) came farming. It is now thought that this revolution began about 10,000 years ago in the 'Fertile Crescent' of present day Lebanon, Israel and Syria. By

Polished flint axe from Breconshire
(acc.no.168 from Brecknock Museum)

around 4000 BC, there is evidence for small garden-style allot-
ments throughout the fertile valleys of western Europe, though
many parts of Britain were still covered by dense wildwood (see
Hodder 1990). By this time, domesticated sheep, continental cattle,
pigs and seed corn had arrived in Britain, now an island. The introduction of agriculture, however, was no 'overnight affair'.
Arguably, a long transitional period began some 3,000 years earlier
during the Mesolithic, with the controlled herding and corralling of
wild animals and the seasonal harvesting of wild fruits, roots and
nuts. By the Late Mesolithic, many of the social and economic
mechanisms for the adoption of agriculture were probably already
in place, such as extended family groups, permanent settlement,
territories, and seasonal hunting and gathering strategies. Due to
poor environmental preservation on Mesolithic sites in
Breconshire, evidence for such mechanisms is difficult to find.
Overall, however, there are clear associations of material evidence
between the Late Upper Palaeolithic/Early Mesolithic and Late
Mesolithic/Early Neolithic, suggesting the transition was more
subtle than was once thought. Although difficult to state for certain,
there is enough evidence to suggest a gradual shift from hunting
and gathering to farming, rather than rapid or revolutionary

A selection of Neolithic flint artefacts from around the Black Mountains, including a blade, three leaf-shaped arrowheads and a scraper (from Brecknock Museum)

economic and social change. At one point, both economies probably operated side-by-side.

Due to the harsh acidic soils in this part of Wales, environmental evidence is minimal. However, some (carbonised) plant remains have been found at a number of Neolithic monuments, including emmer wheat (Gwernvale), hazelnuts (Pipton) and cattle and sheep bones (Gwernvale, Penywyrlod and Ty Isaf). However, it is the pollen record that offers the first indications of agriculture. The presence of plants such as ribwort plantain (*Plantago lanceolata*) are significant, as these usually appear as a result of cultivation or pastoralism. At Llyn Mire, the appearance of ribwort plantain pollen coincides with a decline in elm pollen, suggesting a sequence of woodland clearance followed by cultivation around 3000 BC. Samples taken from 10 sites around Waun Fignen Felen reveal the same pattern of decline and cultivation. As a result of woodland clearance, especially in the Breconshire uplands, blanket peat began to form, a process that continued into the Bronze Age.

Perhaps surprisingly, it is not the economic and settlement evidence that has survived but monuments commemorating the dead. Large megalithic chambered tombs dominate the Neolithic landscape of central Wales (and elsewhere). Originally, these would have been covered by earthen mounds or stone cairns, leaving only

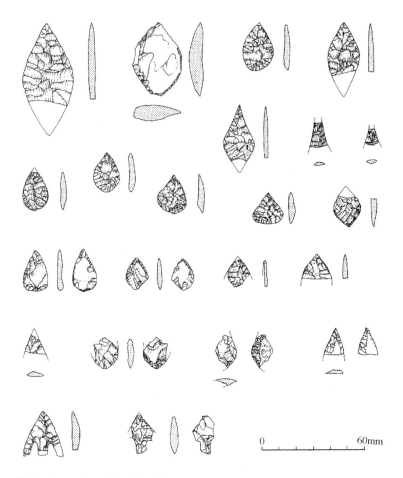

Selection of quality Neolithic lithics including leaf-shaped arrowheads from Gwernvale (from Britnell and Savory 1984)

the entrance and passage visible (see Kinnes 1992). The interior of the tombs, the passage and chamber, is sometimes complex, with certain areas apparently restricted to members of particular social strata. A few of the more impressive monuments around the Black Mountains (Ffostyll North and South, Penywyrlod and Pipton Long Cairn) are intervisible with each other, which means that the people who used them would have been able to see neighbouring tombs in the distance. This suggests that monuments were being sited strategically, not at random (Bradley 1984; Tilley 1994), and that selecting the right location was important. Choosing a site seems to have owed much to tradition, as the association of earlier material with later remains suggests certain places retained a special significance in the minds of our prehistoric ancestors from one 'age' to the next. Gwernvale, where Late Upper Palaeolithic (c.10,000 BC) flint and chert, together with Mesolithic flint, were discovered beneath the monument has already been mentioned. Such sites were clearly being visited by prehistoric communities long before the Neolithic tomb-building phase and may have formed part of a complex communication system connected by ancestral pathways. They may even have served as markers separating territories of neighbouring hunter/gatherer groups. At Gwernvale, evidence of one or perhaps two rectangular wooden structures, indicated by a series of linear post-holes together with construction trenches, was uncovered within the south-eastern part of the tomb and façade area. This has been dated to 3100 BC (dates were taken from a nearby pit within the same archaeological horizon). It has been suggested that the post-hole structure could have been a mortuary platform. Here, the dead would have been laid to rest before bodies were disarticulated and placed within the burial chambers. Associated with this structure was a selection of artefacts, including flint, quern fragments, pottery and cereal grains. Although considered domestic, the items found in association with the post-hole structure may be offerings to the dead.

Gwernvale is one of 23 Neolithic monuments set firmly within a symbolic landscape. The story does not end with the construction of Neolithic chambered tombs, however, as the presence of Bronze Age material indicates an ongoing significance of place. Any one of the Black Mountains sites represents many thousands of years of continuous use, which may have drawn upon a common religious ancestral ideology incorporating both landscape and economic resources, similar to the integral symbolism bound-in with the sacred land rites of the Australian Aborigines.

The careful positioning of our ancestors' monuments in relation to headlands, mountain ridges and river valleys suggests that where the dead were buried was as important as how they were buried. Similar ideas are apparent among contemporary and recent histor-

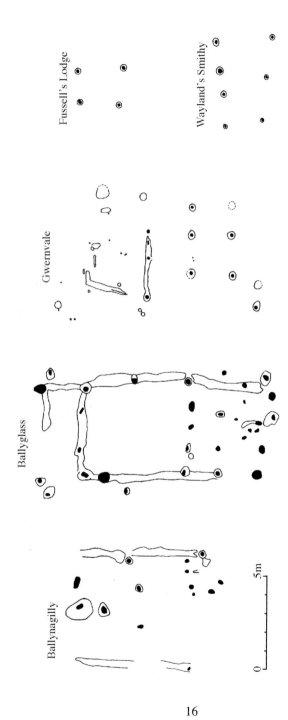

Evidence of wooden mortuary structures from Gwernvale and comparative monuments (from Britnell and Savory 1984)

16

ical societies. The Kunwinjku Aborigines believe certain locations are spiritually powerful because they were created from the vital organs of ancestral beings, the symbolism of the divided body providing the overall conception of landscape in Kunwinjku

Smoking the ancestors: death rituals in Papua New Guinea
(Photograph: Colin Simpson, Courtesy of Angus & Robinson)

17

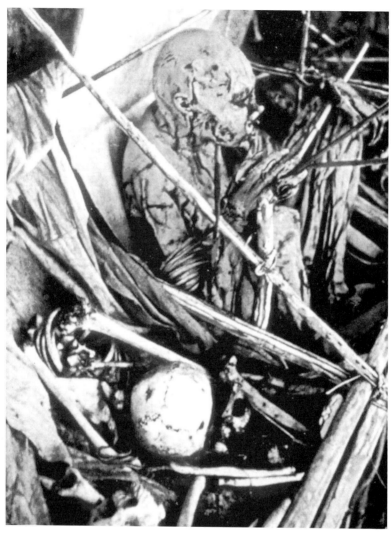

Watching over the living: a smoked corpse sits on a mountain ledge (Photograph: Colin Simpson, Courtesy of Angus & Robinson)

society. It is at these sacred sites that songs and dances are performed to release the spirits of the dead from their bones.

In Victorian England, Highgate Hill in London was chosen as the site of a prestigious cemetery overlooking what was, in the 19th century, the world's largest and most prosperous city. Extending to 17 acres, the cemetery was laid out in such a way that the higher up the hill one's final resting place, the greater one's station in life. Finally, on the summit of Highgate Hill, a series of terraced family vaults embodied a self-contained community of the dead. Here, the wealthy industrialist was assured of a place in posterity (if not necessarily in Heaven) through the sheer monumentality of his mortuary edifice: at the summit of the hill, the dead could never be forgotten. Just as the Victorian industrialist looked out over the metropolis from his vantage point on Highgate Hill, so the Big Men and warriors of the Tauri River, Papua New Guinea, watch over their villages from high mountain ledges. It is the responsibility of kinsmen to smoke-dry fresh corpses inside the hut of the deceased. When the curing is complete, the leathery corpse, now weighing a mere 15-20kg, is carried to the mountains. Here, the corpse is propped up on a ledge with lashed bamboo sticks and arrows and is painted with red ochre (see photos pp.17 & 18). The stance and colour of corpse suggests that the members of the clan group much want him to be alive.

For the Sumba islanders of Indonesia, the coastal locations of their 'houses for the dead' are highly symbolic places, each monument remaining in use for many centuries. Before reaching their final resting place, the dead are paraded through the village and treated with increasing reverence as the procession approaches the stone-chambered tomb.

Similarly, the spatial relationship between Bronze Age stone circles and barrows suggests an initial burial ritual followed by a journey to the place of interment. The Cerrig Duon stone circle (SN 852 206), for example, comprising of a stone circle, large monolith, two stone rows and outlying standing stones all appear to orientate and link into a series of cairns located on or near Mynydd Du, some 2km to the north-west. The linearity of the monuments may suggest the existence of a processional path beginning at the stone circle and terminating at the cairns. If the latter represent journey's end—the final resting place, death—then the stone circle may signify the beginning of that death, a place where the dead could be viewed, a form of 'lying in state' prior to interment.

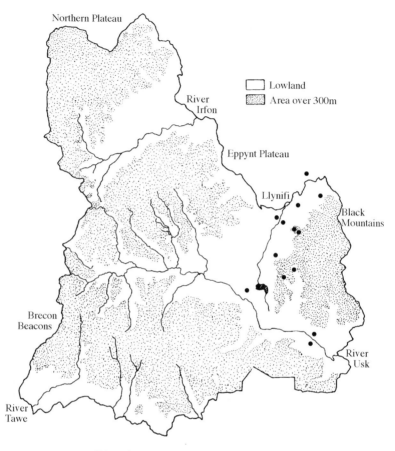

Distribution Map of Neolithic Sites

Territorial Neolithic: The Black Mountains Group

This series of monuments, the only inland group of chambered tombs in Wales, comprises 18 visible structures, 12 in Breconshire, one in Radnorshire (see above map) and five in Herefordshire. The monuments cluster around the Black Mountains, a large, basal sandstone massif of some 35sq. km which forms a boundary between the undulating valleys and lowland pastures of the Welsh Marches and the uplands of central Wales. Early sources suggest there were once as many as 23 monuments around the Dore, Rhiangoll, Usk and Wye valleys (Daniel 1950, Powell *et al.* 1969).

Belonging to the Severn-Cotswold tomb tradition (a phrase first coined by Daniel in 1937), the monuments possess central, terminal and side chambers, a passage, forecourt and, occasionally, a false entrance, all built within an elongated or trapezoidal mound frequently enclosed by drystone walling. Of the 18 monuments remaining, only a handful of forecourts have been fully excavated. Similarities between the Black Mountains group and the Irish 'court tombs' have been noted by the Royal Commission inventory (RCAHM[W] 1997). However, the architecture of court tombs is firmly rooted in the Irish tradition, whereas the Black Mountains monuments exhibit a number of unique characteristics (noted by the authors in 1991 and published as follows: Tilley 1994, Children & Nash 1994 & 1996 and Nash 1997:17-30).

The group extends in an arc around the northern, western and south-western periphery of the Black Mountains. Monuments appear to be locally-oriented, either with the valley or towards prominent features of the immediate landscape (Tilley 1994) and usually occupy the intermediate slopes facing the mountains. Beyond, there appears to be little or no Neolithic activity (Children & Nash 1994:17). A number of tombs are on high upland ridges and plateaus, close to, and in full view of, the mountains. To the north and east, the Wye and Dore provide a focus for eight monuments, including one, Parkwood (1), that is now lost. Some of these are intervisible with other monuments and all are oriented towards local topographic features.

To the south and west, monuments are less dense and follow a different pattern of construction. This may involve development in monument design over time, indicating the importance of particular areas at different times. Some monuments appear to have been in use for long periods. Ty Isaf (13), near Talgarth, and Gwernvale (17), Crickhowell, both reveal evidence of multi-phase building.

Only two tombs, Gwernvale and Carn Goch (18), near Crickhowell, stand close to the flood plain of the lower Usk Valley. Both are set on low ridges: Carn Goch takes Table Mountain (3km to the north-east) as its focus, while Gwernvale is aligned to the River Usk. Of the four passages at Gwernvale, three point towards the Usk and to local spurs and escarpments. The south-eastern passage is slightly angled. A large blocking or doorway stone

Tomb	L	I	U	Metres OD
1. Park Wood		X		200
2. Dunseal Long Barrow			X	175
3. Cross Lodge Barrow		X		180
4. Arthur's Stone			X	280
5. Bach Long Barrow			X	304
6. Court Farm, Clyro	X			90
7. Pen-y-wyrlod			X	250
8. Little Lodge Barrow		X		137
9. Pipton Long Cairn		X		145
10. Ffostyll North			X	312
11. Ffostyll South			X	312
12. Cwm Forest		X		280
13. Ty Isaf		X		310
14. Mynydd Troed			X	358
15. Penywyrlod			X	260
16. Ty Illtyd			X	215
17. Gwernvale	X			79
18. Garn Goch	X			84

L Lowland Position; I Intermediate slope; U Upland

Table indicating landscape position and height above sea level of Neolithic tombs around the edge of the Black Mountains (after Nash 1997)

suggests visual access to the chamber was restricted, while the angled doorway hints at secret ritual-symbolic activity (see below). Similar passage plans exist at Arthur's Stone (4), near Dorstone, and Pipton Long Cairn (9), 5km west of Hay-on-Wye.

On pages 26-39 we have arranged the monuments into six distinct sub-groups (a - f). Each group usually comprises a valley-oriented monument and another aligned with a significant topographic feature. These pairs are separated by rivers and streams, which may have acted as territorial boundaries, although their significance may have been ritual rather than political. For example, Pipton Long Cairn, oriented to the valley (or river) is allied with Little Lodge Barrow (8), located on a west-facing slope and aligned towards the prominent spur Y Das. Set 1.5km apart, the two monuments are separated by the Afon Llynfi.

Name	Parish	Grid Ref	Landscape position	Nearest Tomb
1. Park Wood	St Margarets	35653347	Dore Valley	2
2. Dunseal	Dorstone	39133382	Dore Valley	1
3. Cross Lodge	Dorstone	33254168	Dore Valley	4
4. Arthur's Stone	Dorstone	31804313	Dore Valley	3
5. Bach	Dorstone	27654287	Upper Wye Valley	6
6. Court Farm	Clyro	21234313	Upper Wye Valley	5
7. Pen-y-wyrlod	Llanigon	22483986	Upper Wye Valley	8
8. Little Lodge	Glasbury	18223806	Llynfi Valley	10
9. Pipton	Glasbury	16033728	Llynfi Valley	10
10. Ffostyll North	Llaneliew	17883487	Llynfi Valley	11
11. Ffostyll South	Llaneliew	17883487	Llynfi Valley	10
12. Cwm Forest	Talgarth	18332944	Rhiangoll Valley	13
13. Ty Isaf	Talgarth	18192905	Rhiangoll Valley	12
14. Mynydd Troed	Talgarth	16142843	Llynfi Valley	15
15. Penywyrlod	Talgarth	15053156	Llynfi Valley	14
16. Ty Illtyd	Llanhamlach	9842038	Usk Valley	14
17. Gwernvale	Crickhowell	21111920	Usk Valley	18
18. Garn Goch	Llangattock	21231771	Usk Valley	17

Table indicating location of Neolithic tombs around the edge of the Black Mountains (after Nash 997)

Tombs and the symbolism of the Black Mountains

Mysterious and forbidding, the Black Mountains dominated the Neolithic landscape and acted as a visual magnet. Areas farther east and outside their influence may have been considered dangerous. The mountains too may have been perceived as dangerous and mysterious, as they have yielded very little Neolithic material. Siting a settlement close to, but not actually on the mountains, would create a sense of belonging. In other words, a space would become a place, establishing an identity that, in turn, would create a territory.

Many monuments within the western part of the county are located around the edges of high Neolithic activity. Could these monuments represent territorial markers, as well as providing a place for the dead? Building monuments around the edge of the Golden Valley, for example, would establish a definite territorial area. Very little surface flint has been found immediately outside this area. A similar pattern occurs farther west on Cefn Hill. Here, settlement and monuments appear deliberately oriented towards the Black Mountains.

A number of tombs, including Arthur's Stone in Herefordshire, have produced evidence of a human presence since at least the Late Mesolithic (6000-3500 BC). So, even during the Neolithic, these monuments would have possessed a 'history', an affinity with the ancestors.

To the south-west of Arthur's Stone is Cross Lodge Barrow (SO 333 418), which is easily recognised as it has three large ash trees growing at the southern end of the mound. The two monuments differ in the method of construction. This suggests either that they were built at different times or that they had different meanings, 'meaning' in architecture referring to the expressive or symbolic aspect of a structure rather than its function—an Anglican and a Roman Catholic church are both intended to accommodate religious rituals, but each follows a design code dictated by the particular requirements of the two traditions. Cross Lodge Barrow is aligned with the valley, while Arthur's Stone could be a valley-end marker. The sheer size and weight of the uprights and capstone suggest the latter monument would have consumed a considerable amount of time and the labour of many; a tomb such as this might take up to 16,000 labour hours (between three and seven months) to complete (Startin 1981). The smaller Cross Lodge Barrow, on the other hand, would have involved far less time and effort. Obviously, speed of construction would depend on the accessibility of materials and the availability of labour to haul sandstone blocks across the countryside. Time for tomb-building, perhaps the first task undertaken by settlers staking their claim to a territory, may have been found during the winter months.

Creating metaphors: the architecture of space
The treatment of ancestral remains appears to have been an important element of Neolithic symbolism. At Ty Isaf, near Talgarth, and Parc-le-Breos-Cwm, on the Gower peninsula, bone was disarticulated and segregated according to gender, age, body part and, in some cases, genus. This is only part of a more complex story, however, in which the monument itself, rather than the symbolism

of the human body, takes priority. A symbolic relationship between tomb design and the human body has been suggested (Thomas and Tilley 1994), the internal arrangement of stones representing the rib cage. However, tomb design appears to be in direct conflict with the body for the space is organised so as to oppose body symbolism, hence the necessity to disarticulate the human skeleton. By so doing, the inner space of the tomb is consciously dehumanised, while at the same time the (sacred) knowledge of who the bones belong to is retained. The body has been transformed from something living and recognisable into an object, an artefact (belonging to the ancestors).

Moreover, each monument is organically related to its surroundings. Looking at the remains of a tomb today, only part of the monument is seen—usually a few uprights and a fragmented capstone. This, however, is just the skeleton—angular and mechanical, it stands in stark contrast to the irregular organic forms of the surrounding landscape, suggesting order, control and design. During the Neolithic, this skeleton would have possessed flesh—capstone, uprights and covering stones would all have been hidden from view beneath an earth mound or a covering of smaller stones (cairn), unifying the various structural elements within. While inside nature was rejected in favour of the social and symbolic order, the outer tomb, rather than opposing the landscape, would have formed an integral part with its surroundings.

The American architect Frank Lloyd Wright developed a number of ideas on the use of materials in an organic form which may be applied to mechanical and natural forms in the landscape (Jenks 1969; Frampton 1992; Nash 1997). His Falling Water concept at Bear Run (1936), for example, applies concrete and glass to an organic design. The building incorporates the structural and spatial principles of falling water, in such a way that 'the place of the living is fused into nature' (Frampton 1992). Wright did not believe materials needed to be organic in the true sense of the word, indeed many of his buildings were made from concrete blocks, but it is the way in which the materials are combined that creates organic architecture. It is apparent that the stone frame of the tomb can not be described as organic. These structures are truly mechanical in form. It is only by incorporating these elements within the mound that the monument becomes organic, at one with its surroundings.

Although hidden beneath a mound of earth or stones these structural components remained an important part of the overall tomb concept. The orientation of the monument, the form of the capstone, the position and alignment of the entrance and façade all suggest that the outside is being drawn within. The mechanical structure transforms the inner space of the monument into a stylised ritual map of the surrounding landscape, incorporating significant topographical features. Although the inner space opposes the outer space, the outer space, when replicated within, is manipulated and controlled—the landscape is subdued. Consequently, each monument has developed its own unique morphology. Below eight tombs are considered (Arthur's Stone (4), Pipton (9), Ffostyll North (10) and South (11), Ty Isaf (13), Mynydd Troed (14), Penywyrlod (15) and Gwernvale(17)) to see how these ideas might work in practice. The significant elements appear to be the horns, façade, passages and chambers, which all respond to certain features within their local environment, such as rivers, valley spurs and scarp edges. These monuments are arranged into a series of groups which are geographically clustered within the landscape.

The Dore sub-group (a)
A clear attempt to control landscape can be seen at Arthur's Stone, one of five tombs dominating the northern reaches of the Dore Valley. Set in an oval mound, the monument has nine upright stones supporting a large capstone and, of particular interest, an unorthodox right-angled passage. The south-western end of the capstone points towards the southern part of the Golden Valley, while the chamber has, at its western end, a false portal stone (partly blocking the doorway to the main chamber). The passage starts off in a northerly direction but, mid-way along its length, turns north-west towards Hay Bluff (the northern extent of the Black Mountains). This means that the chamber cannot be seen from the entrance, and *vice versa*. It is as if, by a simple visual device, a conscious attempt is being made to separate human space, the realm of order and control, from the outside world, from nature. The transition between the two is achieved precisely at that point,

equidistant between chamber and entrance, where the passage abruptly changes direction. It is here that human meets nature and order meets disorder. However, this is only part of the meaning behind the monument's construction. The redirection of the passage and the orientation of the capstone suggest Arthur's Stone played a key role in the socio-symbolic process of territory formation. The monument was constructed so as to encompass the entire length of the Black Mountains. In this way, the mountains were incorporated into the social and symbolic identity of these Neolithic settlers, helping to create a sense of belonging. Other tombs in the upper Wye and Usk valleys interact with the landscape in similar ways.

Farther south, down the Dore Valley are three other monuments which suggest that the Neolithic in this area was indeed extensive. The few surface finds suggest a Neolithic or Early Bronze Age date for the Dunseal monument, near Abbeydore. The former is more likely, given the monument's position high on a west-facing ridge, with dominant views to the south and west. Dunseal (2), Garway Common and the now destroyed Parkwood tomb mark the south-ernmost extent of Neolithic influence in the Golden Valley. Beyond, there are no monuments and few artefacts. Together with other tombs around the periphery of the valley, they may have marked out a definite territory, reinforcing a sense of local identity for the valley's inhabitants.

Cross Lodge Barrow (3), located approximately 2km south-east of Arthur's Stone, may have been much larger during the Neolithic. Like Arthur's Stone, the monument has a commanding view of the Black Mountains and would have been visible both from the valley floor and from the substantial Neolithic settlement located on a prominent spur 1km to the north. The tombs, however, are not intervisible.

Farther north, Bach long barrow (5) is the most north-westerly of the Dore Valley Group. Interestingly, it is sited on a north-facing slope, overlooking the upper Wye Valley and not the Dore Valley. Its position suggests, therefore, that it cannot be associated with any of the Golden Valley tombs. The location and localised orientation (east-west) suggest an association with nearby Clyro Court Farm and the now damaged Clyro monuments (see below). All three are in full view of the upper Wye Valley and are intervisible.

As with many other areas of high Neolithic activity, Herefordshire has revealed very little evidence of settlement. However, one notable example was discovered by field-walkers on Dorstone Hill, equidistant between Arthur's Stone and Cross Lodge Barrow. Excavated by Christopher Houlder and Roger Pye between 1965 and 1970, this extensive settlement (SO 326 423) covers approximately 18 acres.

The settlement was enclosed on the west side by a crude stone wall. On top of this wall was a wooden 'stockade'. Also present were storage pits (possibly used for grain), occupation floors and undisturbed 'buried soils', ideal for dating. Fragments of pottery and waste flint were found within this ancient soil, including over 4,000 pieces of flint (many arrowheads) and more than 50 polished stone axe fragments. The stone and flint used to create these prestige items were, in part, imported from as far away as South Wales and the Cotswolds. The contact/exchange of axes between all three areas highlights the importance and prestige of farming groups within the Golden Valley.

The size of the Dorstone settlement suggests that a large population, probably in excess of 250 people, occupied the upland areas of the Golden Valley during the Neolithic, utilising the slopes, ridges and tops of the eastern uplands—from Merbach Hill in the north-east to Canns Hill in the south. By settling on the eastern hills, the community would have lived within full view of the Golden Valley and, more importantly, of the symbolically-significant Black Mountains. Below, the fertile woodland of the valley floor would have been slowly cleared to make way for allotment-style farming. More land would have been brought into production as the population grew. Remaining pockets of woodland scattered throughout the valley would have harboured red deer and wild boar, additional resources that could have been exploited by the Neolithic people in the same way as it had been by their Mesolithic hunting ancestors.

Upper Wye sub-group (b)

This sub-group comprises two monuments sited on the northern intermediate slopes of the River Wye flood plain (two further tombs may have been present during prehistory). All that remains of the

Clyro Court Farm monument is a low mound and a few uprights, the uprights outlining a small chamber and passage. The monument has commanding views across the upper Wye Valley and incorporates the north-western extent of the Black Mountains. The isolated peak of Mynydd Troed can be seen approximately 15km south-south-west at the foot of which several Breconshire tombs are sited, including Mynydd Troed and Penywyrlod. This monument is valley-oriented, the form of the mound governed by the direction of the valley and the course of the Wye (south-west/north-east). Close by, but now destroyed, stood Clyro Long Barrow. In terms of function and meaning, this tomb may have been more akin to Arthur's Stone and Cross Lodge Barrow than to Clyro Court Farm due to its architecture and location high up on the intermediate slopes of Clyro Hill.

Farther west, Little Lodge Barrow stands on a spur that draws together the upper Wye and Llynfi valleys. Excavations by C.E. Vulliamy in 1929 revealed a wealth of artefacts and some human remains. The mound, now much disturbed, is oriented north-south and has two, or perhaps three, chambers present — a simple terminal chamber, the remains of a lateral chamber that opens out from the west and possibly a third chamber which is now marked by a single upright at the northern end. The mound is oriented north/south with the impressive Hay Bluff in full view. In addition, there is inter-visibility with Pipton Long Cairn (8), 2.3km due west.

Llynfi sub-group (c)

Farther west, close to Talgarth, a series of monuments cluster around the Afon Llynfi. These monuments arguably form the core of the main group. The largest, most impressive and, standing 310m OD, the highest monuments in the Black Mountains group, are Ffostyll North, oriented east-west, and the north-south aligned Ffostyll South. Ffostyll South, the smallest and best-preserved of the two, has a single gallery-type chamber located at its north-eastern end. Two dislodged capstones are supported by ten uprights. The larger northern mound is considered multi-phase and possibly trapezoidal in plan (Corcoran 1969). The mound incorporates three chambers: a destroyed eastern chamber plus two others located centrally and at the south-western end. There is no evidence of passages.

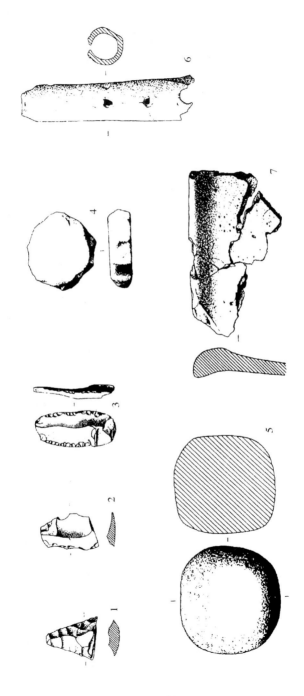

Artefacts found at Penywyrlod, Talgarth, include: 1-3 lithics, 4-5 stone tools, 6 bone flute and 7 pottery (from Britnell and Savory 1984)

Both Ffostyll North and South have commanding views to the south-west and may have been intervisible with Penywyrlod. Directly to the south and east, Ffostyll North appears to be aligned to the dominant spurs of Y Das and Rhia y Fan, whereas Ffostyll South is aligned with the valley and the nearby Afon Ennig. Two small tributaries close by run westwards into the Ennig. The northern mound, the east/west orientation of which suggests a link with the rising and setting of the sun and, by extension the life/death cycle, is sited slightly higher up the slope than Ffostyll South which is orientated north/south and may be considered the more dominant and earlier of the two.

Approximately 3.5km to the north is Penywyrlod. This tomb is constructed of four uprights and retains traces of an elongated (pear-shaped) mound, approximately 18.5m long and oriented south-west/north-east with the valley. The uprights form a small rectangular terminal chamber. At the north-eastern end of the mound are traces of a small chambered structure. The tomb may in fact be multi-phased (Corcorcan 1969) and, if so, Penywyrlod may have been in use over a long period. The tomb is located on a high truncated spur overlooking the Wye and Llynfi valleys, but has no direct intervisibility with Clyro Court Farm (3.5km), Little Lodge (4.7km) or Pipton Long Cairn (7km).

Pipton Long Cairn, one of four 'hybrid' Severn-Cotswold monuments within this group, is located on an east-facing slope overlooking the north-western extent of the Black Mountains. By 'hybrid' it is meant that a monument has distinctive characteristics such as a trapezoidal mound, side entrances, sometimes a false portal and a horned façade. The mound, 32m long, was constructed with a drystone revetment wall and is oriented north/south, overlooking the upper reaches of the Wye. There are many similarities between this monument and others within the Black Mountains Group. Thus, the northern chamber and passage arrangement is identical to that of Arthur's Stone (Houlder 1978, Castleden 1992). The west-facing passage is angled in two places concealing the chamber from the outside world. The outer cairn shape and architecture includes a trapezoidal mound with extended rounded horns and a false portal (constructed of two uprights). These features are also found at Penywyrlod, Ty Isaf and Gwernvale. A second chamber, south-west facing, has no passage, but an earlier phase of construction has been recognised suggesting a passage would not be required (Castleden 1992). The plan indicates a similarity with the multi-phase construction at Ty Isaf. Disarticulated human bone fragments were found inside the chamber, the bone probably coming from elsewhere (Houlder 1978) suggesting that Pipton was either a final resting place for the dead (the bones) or that it may have served as a temporary abode.

Topographically, the setting is similar to that of other nearby tombs. Ffostyll North and South and Little Lodge appear to point to corresponding features within the landscape—the spurs of Y Das and Hay Bluff. This small cluster of monuments are also intervisible with each other—from Pipton, Penywyrlod, Ffostyll North and South and Little Lodge Barrow can be clearly seen and may constitute a territory.

Penywyrlod long cairn had been quarried for hardcore before being 'discovered' and excavated by Herbert Savory in 1972. However, much of the chamber and passage plan at the southern end of the mound remains intact. Originally, Penywyrlod possessed two extended horns and a false portal at the southern end. Also present are three chambers with disturbed capstones and the remains of two passages. Both chambers and passages look out towards the Black Mountains, even though, to the west, the Brecon Beacons are in full view and it would appear that the internal architecture is concerned only with the Black Mountains. This monument is clearly valley aligned, even though oriented towards Mynydd Troed. The mound, now much disturbed, is aligned north/south and its three chambers comprise a simple terminal chamber, the remains of a lateral chamber that opens out from the west and a possible third chamber, now marked by a single upright at the northern end. Although the mound is oriented north/south, the impressive Hay Bluff is in full view.

One monument that deserves a passing mention but no longer exists is the Bryn y Groes or Croesllechau burial chamber once located near the small village of Pontithel, between Talgarth and Three Cocks (SO 1672 3626), a monument pictorially recorded by Theophilus Jones in his *A History of Brecknock* (1809) (see opposite). The site was also visited by Edward Lhuyd in 1700 who made

Croesllechau. Engraving from Theophilus Jones'
A History of Brecknock *(1809)*

a series of annotated sketches. Based entirely upon his sketches, the site appears to have possessed a rectangular chamber, delineated by five uprights, a supporting capstone and possibly a false portal. The latter architectural feature suggests that this monument may have been trapezoidal in form, similar to nearby Pipton Long Cairn and thus belonging to the Severn-Cotswold tradition of monuments. The site recorded by Jones shows a large, roughly cut capstone, which probably would have been of Old Red Sandstone. Beneath the capstone appear to be two supporting orthostats. It is probable that the monument was destroyed sometime during the first decade of the 19th century. According to the RCHAM(W) and antiquarian notes, the location of the monument is now unknown. The general landscape position of this monument is set within a valley, close to the Afon Llynfi and may have had similar landscape orientation and architectural affinities as Gwernvale. It is more than probable that it would have possessed direct intervisiblity with Pipton Long Cairn.

33

The Llangors/Honddu sub-group (d)

Farther west are two monuments that appear to ignore the influence of the Black Mountains. Both have commanding views over the Brecon Beacons and lowland pastures of Llyn (lake) Llangors and Afon Honddu. Mynydd Troed (14), which stands at the foot of the Mynydd Troed peak, is one of the least impressive mounds, yet it is set in one of the most dramatic of all Black Mountains landscapes. Lying between Mynydd Troed and Mynydd Llangors, the monument faces south-east towards Cwm Sorgwm and Pen Allt-mawr. It also has views to the west, towards Llyn Llangors. Both Mynydd Troed and another monument, Ty Illtyd (16), are sited around 3.5km from Llyn Llangors and may be linked territorially. The area around the mound may have marked the transition from open scrub to woodland, (Grimes 1932; 1936a) and, if so, the mound would have been concealed from view, in spite of standing well over 254m OD. However, visibility may have been enhanced by clearing a swathe of vegetation from around the monument.

The oval mound is oriented north-east/south-west and encloses a simple terminal chamber and at least one other, but recent disturbance makes reconstruction near-impossible. However, Mynydd

Ty Illtyd. An engraving of 1887 by Henry Longueville
(*from* Archaeologia Cambrensis)

Troed does resemble other monuments within the overall group, notably Penywyrlod, Ffostyll North and Ty Illtyd.

Outside the main group, but possibly associated with Mynydd Troed, is the isolated Ty Illtyd (see opposite). Positioned on a west-facing ridge approximately 6.6km due west of Mynydd Troed, Ty Illtyd incorporates a visual setting that includes the eastern portion of the Brecon Beacons. Both chamber and capstone are aligned towards Pen y Fan, the highest point in the Beacons. The monument comprises a single capstone overlying a rectangular chamber, delineated by eight uprights, and is set into a raised oval earth mound. The mound and chamber are oriented north/south with a small rectangular forecourt or antechamber at the northern end which has been interpreted as a second chamber (Corcoran 1969).

Rhiangoll sub-group (e)
On the eastern side of Mynydd Troed stand a further three monuments of which Ty Isaf is the largest and most complex. Excavated in 1938, Ty Isaf is regarded as a 'hybrid' Severn-Cotswold tomb. Typically, it has a complex series of chambers and passages within a trapezoidal plan (oriented north/south), a false doorway and extended horns and façade. Although complex in plan, all that remains of this monument are a few protruding orthostats and the remnants of the elongated mound (30m x 18m). However, the landscape setting can be regarded as an important element of the overall meaning behind its location and architecture.

The plan reveals at least three phases of construction and use. Phase I comprises a small, oval cairn structure at the southern end of the mound, measuring 12m in diameter and containing a south-east-facing passage and a chamber oriented south-west/north-east. This structure may have been additional to the larger mound plan, (Corcoran 1969) however it is more likely to be the earliest structure, the larger trapezoidal mound being added later (Castleden 1992). The main mound structure (Phase II), has two chambers (with passages), and a curious false doorway. The mound itself is of a double drystone revetment wall. The actual doorway is located at the northern end, between two horns. The plan and orientation is very similar to another 'hybrid' tomb in this group: Pipton Long Barrow. Both the west and east lateral passages look out towards dominant topographic features: Mynydd Troed to the west and Waun Fach to the east, whilst approximately 100m west is the southward-flowing Afon Rhiangoll. These features may be regarded as necessary symbolic components of the overall plan and shape of Ty Isaf.

Approximately 300m to the north are the remains of Cwm Fforest (or Cwmfforest) (12). Here, according to Crawford (1925:54-55) the chamber is of drystone walling with a capstone set centrally within a small south-east/north-west mound, at the south-eastern end of which was once a passage (Corcoran 1969). Like Ty Isaf, Cwm Fforest stands within a dramatic valley/pass location and may have been architecturally similar to its neighbour (Castleden 1992). Both tombs may well have been in use at the same time, but, like Ffostyll North and South, serving different needs.

The more complex architecture of Ty Isaf includes passages and chambers aligned with steep mountain slopes to the west and mountain spurs to the south and east. Moreover, the overall orientation of the plan appears to be influenced by the Afon Rhiangoll, while the original form of the mound may have echoed the surrounding mountain peaks. The tomb may thus be seen as a 'compass', a central point in the landscape, the chambers aligned east-west to catch the rising and setting of the sun, perhaps representing the cycle of life and death (see Bourdieu 1990). At Ffostyll South, the cairn is remarkably similar in form to the peak of Mynydd Troed, when looking towards the south-west. The same is true of Penywyrlod, where tomb orientation betrays the influence of the River Llynfi and the two chambers point towards Y Das and Hay Bluff at the northern end of the Black Mountains. No passages or chambers occur on the west side of tomb, which is in full view of the Brecon Beacons. Ty Isaf, Ffostyll South and other monuments in the group are not man-made structures proclaiming opposition to the landscape, but are themselves very much a part of that landscape.

The Lower Usk sub-group (f)

The two chambered tombs of Gwernvale and Garn Coch are sited on low ridges above the flood plains on each side of the River Usk, north-west and south-east of Crickhowell respectively. One of the more impressive and most important monuments in this part of

Gwernvale showing blocking of passages to chambers 1, 2 and 3 (Britnell and Savory 1984)

Wales, Gwernvale, excavated in 1978, is of rubble infill supported by drystone walling and is similar in design to others within the main group. Of the four passages, three point towards the Usk and local spurs and escarpments. The south-eastern passage is slightly deflected by a large blocking stone, which suggests restricted visual access. The elongated mound, constructed of a double revetment wall, is oriented east/west. Traces of an ancient cement were found between the uprights and the drystone walling during the 1977-78 excavation (Britnell 1979). Upper Palaeolithic flint suggests the site was visited over thousands of years and may have marked the convergence of a series of ancestral pathways. If so, this may have been the reason the Neolithic community built its monument where it did.

At the eastern end are two 'horns' and a false portal. Two lateral chambers at the southern end of the mound are clearly visible. The largest is polygonal and comprises six substantial uprights. A passage opens out towards a number of lowland topographic features in the south-west including the River Usk and Mynydd Llangatwg. A third chamber has been badly damaged and there is a further small, single chamber on the northern side. Investigations revealed very few human remains. However, much material was removed during an earlier excavation in 1804, furthermore, Gwernvale suffered considerable damage as a result of road widening on the A40. The 1978 excavation did, however, reveal six large post holes in the forecourt area, suggesting some type of shrine or mortuary house.

Located on a small rise overlooking the River Usk and mountains to the north and south, Garn Goch has an identical landscape setting. The form of the monument is difficult to determine. The oval mound has its northern end towards Table Mountain, a prominent truncated spur on the southern edge of the Black Mountains. Garn Goch has been variously defined as a long cairn, possibly similar to nearby Gwernvale (Crawford 1925; Grimes 1936a and 1936b), and as a simple cist or round mound (Daniel 1950). Large stones 'placed' on top of the mound delineate a simple rectangular chambered struc-ture. Many of the traits attributed to other monuments in this region, such as topographic orientation, also apply here.

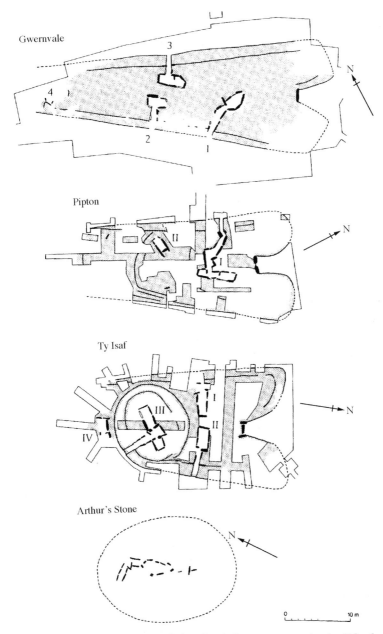

*Comparative sizes of Neolithic burial monuments in the Black
Mountains group (from Britnell and Savoury 1984)*

A theory behind Neolithic landscapes

People's perception of certain objects within their surroundings is of fundamental importance in establishing a sense of belonging. However, a single focal point such as a monument is not sufficient in itself to enable an individual to construct, cognitively and visually, a complete landscape. Many other components are required — in this case valley spurs, rivers, scarp edges, slopes — in order to create a visual totality. By incorporating these components, tomb space becomes an integral part of a greater space, the landscape. The tomb does not have to be monumental in order to make a statement of ownership and control upon this landscape; there need only be the consciousness of monumentality, something which is controlled and manipulated by knowledge — ritual knowledge. The French architect Le Corbusier established the idea that architecture is not a physical medium but a conscious awareness of concept, design and ideology. He states:

> ... By the use of inert materials and starting from conditions more or less utilitarian, you have established certain relationships which have aroused my emotions. This is Architecture.

These emotions constitute what we may term a 'sense of belonging'. Although meaning is shared, the concept of meaning is complex, in that individuals and groups share the same concept, *i.e.* architectural form (Jenks 1969:13). This adds complexity to the visuality of monuments within landscape. In other words, the individual creates his or her own story and the monument becomes an object for all who perceive it. To the archaeologist, it is merely a site. To our Neolithic ancestors, it represented a multitude of different meanings, symbols of individuality and restricted significance — various people within a group having access to different parts of the monument.

NOTE: Monuments numbers 1 to 6 form part of the same group of tombs that are found in Breconshire, but as they lie in Herefordshire and Radnorshire are not included in the following section. However, they are briefly described in Appendix II.

Little Lodge Barrow (7)

Neolithic long barrow
Location: 1km south of Three Cocks, nr. Glasbury (SO 182 380)
Access: On private land, but can be seen from the road

In Three Cocks, on the A438 between Hay and Brecon, head east towards Hay. Just outside the village, take the first right signposted 'Llanigon'. Continue along the lane for about 1km and Little Lodge Barrow can clearly be seen sited between two orchard trees, 320m south of Little Lodge Farm. Permission is required from the nearby farm before visiting this monument.

Excavated in 1929 by C.E. Vulliamy, Little Lodge Barrow, which has been severely disturbed, including the chamber areas, by tree-root damage, has revealed many unburned human remains and charcoal flecks, and bones of red deer, a sheep and cattle. It was estimated that the human remains represented five adult males, an elderly female and perhaps three children. However, a re-evaluation of the material by a team from the British Museum possibly indicates four adults and one youth (all male). Also included within the re-examination was a single red deer molar which appeared to be notched. These were all found in a chamber complex just south of the mound centre. The mound, now destroyed, is oriented north/south and has two or maybe three chambers present: a simple terminal chamber, the remains of a lateral chamber that opens out from the west and, possibly, a third chamber which is now marked by a single upright at the northern end. The RCAHM(W) report (1997) identifies a complex chamber structure located 7m from the southern terminal point of the mound. This consists of 12 uprights delineating a complex chamber alignment. The mound is possibly a typical Severn-Cotswold type with a horned façade area in the northern section. The chamber, possibly entered from side passages on the western side of the mound, suggests that a false portal or entrance was located at the northern end, an architectural detail similar to that of Pipton Long Cairn. Both chamber and passage would have had extensive views across the upper Wye Valley. The hurried excavation by Vulliamy did not establish a clear architectural form for this monument and we suspect that he was only interested in the contents of the cham-

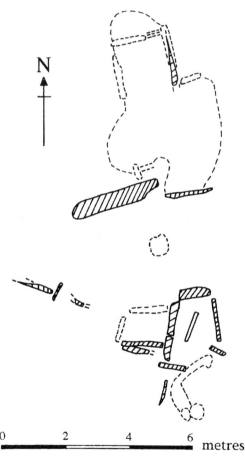

Little Lodge Barrow. Detail of central chamber area (adapted from RCAHM[W])

bers. External architectural detail may survive on the western side of the mound.

Although the mound is oriented north/south, the impressive Hay Bluff is in full view. In addition, there is intervisibility with Pipton Long Cairn, 2.3km due west. Located on a west-facing slope above the Afon Llynfi, approximately 130m OD on a small platform 56m long x 22m wide (17m at the south end), the tomb appears to be aligned to Hay Bluff, rather than valley orientated, although a small stream does flow close by. Over the recent past, the eastern side of the mound has been subjected to ploughing, as well as being robbed for building stone. On the western side the mound is protected by a hedge boundary which severely slopes away to the west in the next field and the height of the mound stands at 1.8m.

Little Lodge with Hay Bluff to the right of the picture

Pen-y-Wyrlod (8)

Neolithic long barrow
Location: South-west of Hay, towards Llanigon (SO 224 398)
Access: On private land, though a public footpath runs close by

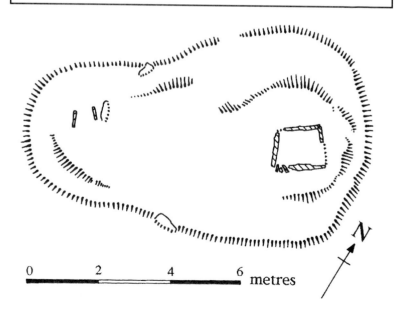

0   2   4   6 metres

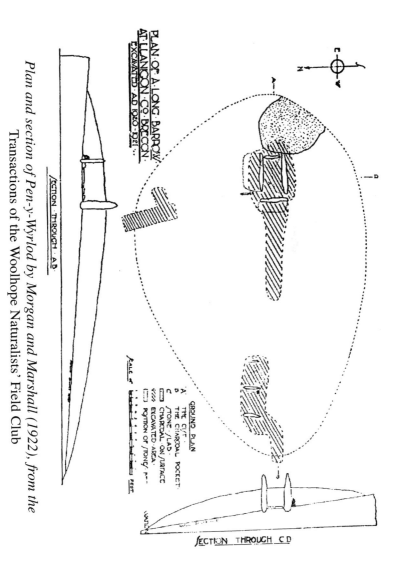

PLAN · OF · A · LONG · BARROW
AT · LLANGON · CO · BRECON ·
EXCAVATED · AD · 1920 · 1921 ·

SECTION · THROUGH · A · B ·

GROUND · PLAN
A   THE · CUT ·
B   THE · CHARCOAL · POCKET ·
C   STONE · SLAB ·
      CHARCOAL · ON · SURFACE ·
      EXCAVATED · AREA ·
      PORTION · OF · STONE · ■

SCALE

FEET

SECTION · THROUGH · C · D

Plan and section of *Pen-y-Wyrlod* by Morgan and Marshall (1922), from the
Transactions of the Woolhope Naturalists' Field Club

45

From Hay-on-Wye, take the mountain road to Abergavenny (first turning left off the B4350). Take the first right along a narrow lane. Proceed for approximately 2km and Pen-y-Wyrlod is located on a field boundary on the right, about 100m from the lane, near where a public footpath is signposted from the road. If you walk up this path, the barrow will be seen to your left.

All that survives of this tomb is a series of four uprights and traces of an elongated (pear-shaped) mound approximately 18.5m in length, the uprights forming a small rectangular terminal chamber. At the north-eastern end of the mound are traces of a small chambered structure. Corcorcan (1969) suggests that the tomb is a multi-phase structure and therefore in use over a long period of time. Its position within the landscape also suggests a symbolic strategic importance in that the orientation of the mound (south-west/north-east) is the same as that of the upper Wye Valley. In addition, the tomb is located on a high truncated spur and there-fore commands views right across the Wye and Llynfi valleys, although it does not have any direct intervisibility with the Clyro Court Farm monument (3.5km), Little Lodge Barrow (4.7km) or Pipton Long Barrow (7km).

The monument was originally excavated between 1920 and 1921 by Rev. W.E.T. Morgan and George Marshall (and members of the Woolhope Naturalists' Field Club). Very little in the way of artefacts was found except for a few fragments of 'rough pottery and a few flint flakes'. The excavation methodology subsequently came under much criticism and the spoil heaps were later investi-gated by C.E. Vulliamy and later still by Gwynne. Between them they found flint, traces of Beaker pottery, a Roman coin (dated AD 317-26) and a large quantity of blue glass beads from what was believed to be an early (possibly 6th century) Anglo-Saxon burial.

Pipton Long Cairn (9)

Neolithic long barrow
Location: Between Hay and Glasbury (SO 160 372)
Access: On private land but permission may be obtained
from the farm

From Glasbury travel along the A438 for approximately 3km to the hamlet of Pontithel. From Pontithel, continue westwards for 1km and take first the narrow farm track on the right to Trevithel Farm. Once you have permission from the farm, walk due north across three fields. Pipton Long Cairn is located in the corner of an east-facing field. It is recognised by a single upright and disturbed cairn material.

Pipton Long Cairn, one of four 'hybrid' Severn-Cotswold monuments within this group, lies 150m above sea level on an east-facing slope overlooking the north-western extent of the Black Mountains. The siting of the monument also divides the River Wye from its tributary the Afon Llynfi. Pipton's mound, once covered with trees, is 37m in length and 22m wide. It was constructed of a

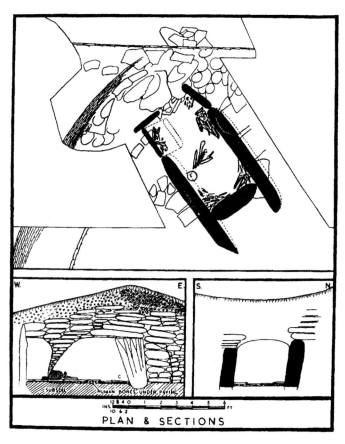

PLAN & SECTIONS

Plan of the chamber area
(from Archaeologia Cambrensis *100:1949)*

drystone revetment wall, information first published in 1925. The tomb was excavated by Herbert Savory in 1949. The mound is oriented north/south and overlooks the upper reaches of the River Wye and shares many similarities with other monuments within the Black Mountains Group. For example, Pipton's northern chamber (Chamber 1), T-shaped in design, and passage arrangement is identical to that of Arthur's Stone (Houlder 1978, Castleden 1992). The west-facing passage, which is central within the cairn fabric, is angled in two places with two door stones, thus making any visibility between the outside and the chamber impossible. In plan, the entrance to the passage, entered from the north side, includes a small sill comprising a series of upright slabs and is narrower than the central and deeper sections of the passage. Headroom within the main chamber area (also referred to as 'the gallery') was found to be 1.3m, similar to Arthur's Stone. The chamber is divided into two sections: the north transept measured 3.5m x 1m and was further sub-divided by a door stone halfway along its length; the smaller south transept, measuring 1m x 0.8m was also blocked with a single door stone slab. The outer cairn, which according to RCAHM(W) (1997) originally attained a height of nearly 2m, and the architecture included a trapezoidal (wedge-shaped) mound with extended rounded horns and a false portal (constructed of two uprights). These features are also present at Pen-y-Wyrlod, Ty Isaf and Gwernvale. A second chamber measuring 1.9m x 1m. internally is south-west facing and has no passage, but Castleden (1992) recognised an earlier 'cultural' phase of construction and therefore a passage would not be required. It is suggested that this structure may be a closed cist so entry would have been from above. However, it would appear that a phase of this monument — a circular structure at the terminal end — may have existed similar to that of the circular mound at Ty Isaf. This feature is recognised as an internal revetment wall, but, in its present form, its function is unknown. The perimeter may also have incorporated the other passage with the chamber acting as the passage rather than the passage being the chamber. The plan suggests a similarity with the multi-phase construction at Ty Isaf. At the terminal part of the mound, on the south-western side, are two canted slabs which were probably used in some earlier architecture of the monument.

Prior to the construction of the monument, the ground had been carefully prepared. On the southern side, earth had been scooped away to create a level surface and within this context were found charcoal and sandstone chips which, according to the RCAHM(W) (1997), related to the building process. However, the charcoal may represent part of the ritual process of the building of the monument. Also present was a single piece of unidentifiable Neolithic pottery. Savory also noted that this surface had a number of marker stones which delineated this section of the monument. These uprights stood shallow within the soil horizon and would not have possessed any structural purpose. Similar to other monuments within the group, the chambers were surrounded by a cairn consisting of angular sandstone blocks and flags. Also present were water-rolled blocks and pebbles which were possibly brought up from the nearby Afon Llynfi. The trapezoidal shape of the mound is supported by two or more revetment walls that may represent different phases of building. Like many other monuments in the Severn-Cotswold group, there appears to have been a need to enlarge the monument in order to impress (see also the plan of Ty Isaf). The inner revetment appears to be constructed in coarser fashion than the outer, and the revetment wall in places was constructed of 24 courses rising to a height of 0.75m. An alternative interpretation for this wall is structural rather than aesthetic.

Present within the main chamber was an incomplete assemblage of disarticulated human bone beneath the floor slabs of the south transept, as well as human and animal bone and a flint flake within the passage area. Houlder (1978) suggests that the bone had probably come from elsewhere. Pipton may either, therefore, have been the final resting place for the dead or it may have 'acted' merely as an interim resting place. Within the second chamber were also deposits of human bone beneath the floor, and there were seven groups of human bone placed against the side walling of the chamber. Covering the bone was a layer of earth which may have been introduced ritually, thus not only interring the dead within the monument but also burying and hiding them from the living. A similar sequence can be argued for the way the dead are 'buried' in Madagascar. Not only are they interred within a chambered mausoleum but they are wrapped within a cloth (lamba cloth), within which they are allowed to decompose. The decomposition and putrefaction process is thus hidden from the living.

The topography surrounding Pipton is similar to that of other nearby tombs. Both Ffostyll North and South, Little Lodge Barrow, as well as Pipton appear to point to corresponding features within the landscape—the spurs of Y Das and Hay Bluff. This small cluster of monuments within the group also share a common inter-visibility with each other—from Pipton, Penywyrlod, Ffostyll North and South, and Little Lodge Barrow can be clearly seen. Arguably, this cluster may constitute a territory.

Ffostyll North & South (10/11)

Pair of Neolithic long barrows
Location: In Llaneliew parish, to the east of Talgarth
(SO 178 348)
Access: On private land, but permission may be gained
from the farm

Ffostyll North and South lie approximately 70m apart. Both are located in a field 200m north of Ffostyll Farm. Drive through Talgarth on the A479 towards Abergavenny and take the first turning left. Then take the second left turning past the church up a narrow lane. Ffostyll Farm lies 3km up this road on the left. Permission is required from the farm when visiting these monuments.

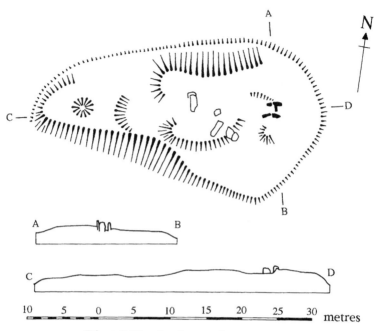

Ffostyll North, plan and cross-section

In 1842, the Rev. T. Price wrote 'the most notable grave mounds I saw in Wales are in the parish of Llanelieu, Breconshire, on the land of the farm called Ffos-t-yll. The biggest of these mounds is 45 yards [41m] long, 20 yards [18m] wide and about two yards [1.8m] high; and they showed that they were full of cistvaens [cists] of the same size - one of which was lately broken for the sake of the stones. There are still enough left to show its size and its workmanship. It was 10 feet [3m] long, five feet [1.5m] wide and eight feet [2.4m] deep, formed of great stones one at each end and two at each side and covered with corresponding stones.' (Hanes Cymru 1842:32).

Both monuments were partially investigated between 1921-23 by C.E. Vulliamy. The Ffostyll North mound is oriented east/west, while the Ffostyll South mound runs north/south. The orientation of the northern mound is significant to the symbolism linked to the life/death (east/west) cycle. Therefore, it would appear that the mounds are in direct opposition with each other (Vulliamy 1923). Ffostyll South, the smallest and best preserved of the two, has a single 3m gallery-type chamber located at the north-eastern end.

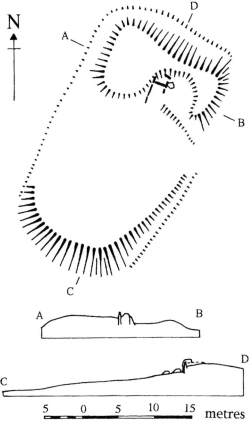

Ffostyll South. Plan and cross-section

Two dislodged capstones are supported by ten uprights. According to Vulliamy both mounds had been disturbed. He remarks: 'At first glance the southern one appeared to have suffered a more searching devastation. Here I found that a vast amount of stone had been moved from the southern end, and there was considerable disturbance which I expected to contain the principal cist. Furthermore, a large covering stone lay tilted on the face of the mound. On examination, I came to the conclusion that neither of these disturbances had touched the burial chamber, which, though its form was not clear, was traceable in the centre of the highest part of the barrow. From information supplied by Mr Gwillym the tenant of the farm I learned that the stone had been removed from the lower southern end of the barrow about forty-five years ago [c.1875], to supply material for road-making; and at that time quantities of human bone had come to light.'

The southern monument was excavated in September 1921 and lasted a mere four days! What was uncovered was an entire cist with roofing slab. Within the lower stratigraphy of the cist was a layer of burnt bone, mainly small fragments which could not be properly identified, though it was ascertained to be the remains of domesticated animals, such as goat, oxen and pig. Around a third of

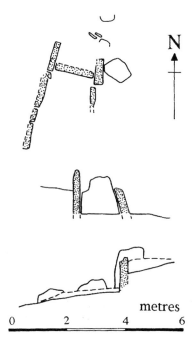

*Ffostyll South. Detailed plan
and cross-section
of the chamber*

a metre below this layer was a considerable amount of human bone which was scattered throughout the length of the chamber. According to Vulliamy: 'The bones were in the utmost confusion; only in a few instances were they in anatomical relation to each other, and by far the greater number were split and broken'. Some of the bones were wedged between the surrounding stones. Human remains included 70 fragments of crania and lower jaw (mandible), 36 metacarpals, metatarsals and phalanges, 6 vertebrae, 30 detached teeth, 135 fragments of long bone and 240 unidentified fragments, including non-human remains. According to the osteology, two unusual characteristics were noted: an adult skull was recovered which was interpreted as being elongated, and a male frontal bone with strong brow ridges. It was concluded that the bone material represented at least nine individuals of both sexes and of various ages. Sir Arthur Keith, Royal College of Surgeons, commenting on the pathology of the bones, suggested that the material was typical of an ancient date (it must be remembered that radiocarbon dating was not available during the 1920s). He deduced that one of the cranial fragments belonged to a male aged about 40 and another was the lower mandible of an (old) woman. Among the remains were also fragments of a cremated youth and a young child, aged 6, as well as the tibia of a seven-month-old foetus. Vulliamy estimated the average stature of adult males was only 5ft. 4ins. (1.62m) tall. No traces of pottery were discovered, but three pieces of flint were found in the cist.

In the following season Vulliamy excavated the chamber at the northern end and revealed more cremated remains including those of one adult and a very young child, plus a pig or goat. Also recovered were fragments of crude, black pottery (later interpreted as the remains of 'a round-bottomed bowl of Neolithic A type' [early undecorated cooking ware]) and 17 pieces of flint and chert, all of which had been immersed in fire (1923:320-324). Vulliamy noted that there was a surprisingly low number of vertebrae present within the skeletal assemblage. Indeed, a large percentage of bone material was absent which may suggest Ffostyll South (and North) may have been the final resting place for the ancestors after their removal from other sites.

A similar argument is put forward by Colin Renfrew (1979) at the Quanterness monument in Orkney, whereby he argues ancestral bones were being moved from tomb to tomb

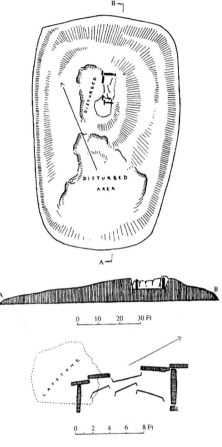

Ffostyll South. Plan and section from Vulliamy's excavation notes (from Archaeologia Cambrensis *76:1921)*

and were eventually deposited in the largest monument within a specified group. Interestingly, both Ffostyll North and South are the largest and most visible monuments within the Black Mountains group, as well as occupying the highest location (312m OD).

The larger northern mound is considered to be a multi-phased monument, possibly trapezoidal in plan (Corcoran 1969). The mound, which has been denuded by excavation and livestock

Late Neolithic/Early Bronze Age Pygmy cup from Ffostyll South (from Brecknock Museum)

erosion, incorporates three chambers: a destroyed eastern chamber that consisted of five upright stones of local sandstone, with no surviving capstone, plus two others, located centrally and at the south-western end. Unfortunately, there is no evidence of any passages leading from any of the three chambers. The main chamber contained human remains as well as those of horse, dog, ox and pig. They were found in undisturbed deposits and were spread along the chamber floor, some retaining their correct anatomical relationship. Among the human bones were those belonging to two children, aged 6 and 11. Sir Arthur Keith, responsible for the osteology, also noted the vertebra of a rheumatoid arthritic female and the mandible of a large male, as well as a number of hand and foot bones. Also recovered were flint flakes and pottery.

Both Ffostyll North and South have commanding views towards the south-west and may be intervisible with Penywyrlod. Directly to the south and east, Ffostyll North appears to be aligned to the dominant spurs of Y Das and Rhia y Fan, whereas Ffostyll South is aligned to the valley and the nearby Afon Ennig (2.5km). Two small tributaries close to both tombs run westwards into the Ennig. The northern mound is sited slightly higher up the slope than Ffostyll South and therefore may be considered the more dominant and possibly much earlier of the two. Irrespective of size, both monuments, although directly opposing one another due to mound orientation, could also be considered as harmonisation in that they encompass the four major directions and thus a complete landscape.

Cwmfforest (12)

Neolithic long barrow
Location: In the hamlet of Cwmfforest near Talgarth
(SO 183 294)
Access: On private land

This monument, considered to be partially destroyed, is sited approximately 300m north of Ty Isaf, close to the Afon Rhiangoll. Visibly all that remains today is drystone walling and a large capstone (possibly *in situ*). Crawford, who visited the site with Mortimer Wheeler in 1924 (1925:54-55), complained that the monument was very difficult to find and its whereabouts had to be pointed out by the owner of Ty Isaf Farm. At that time it was hidden in a 'dense thicket of brambles and young saplings' (*ibid.* 54). Crawford claims that the chamber, which he said was exposed at the south-eastern end of the mound, was constructed from drystone walling with the capstone set over the chamber—both are centrally placed within a small south-east/north-west mound. The south-eastern end of the mound is narrower and Crawford felt it may have formed an entrance passage to the chamber, an observation that has subsequently been reinforced (Corcoran 1969). A steep ditch or gully lies parallel to the mound and within it are a number of cairn stones which probably formed part of the outer covering of the monument.

Cwmfforest shares the same landscape as Ty Isaf, that of a dramatic valley/pass location. It has been suggested that Cwmfforest may have a similar architecture to its neighbour (Castleden 1992). This being the case the authors would suggest that both tombs could well have been in use at the same time, but, like Ffostyll North and South, each served different social and symbolic obligations to their communities.

The recent RCAHM(W) volume (1997:65) suggests that the Cwmfforest monument is in fact a corn-drying kiln which is constructed of a 'rectangular kiln chamber and low, slab-roofed flue passage facing into the river gorge below'. However, conversations with local landowners cannot recall the structure having been ever used as a corn drying kiln. Furthermore, it should be noted that with the altitude of this monument at *c.*260m OD and local land use devoted mainly to sheep grazing, it is unlikely that any corn was dried within the immediate area.

Ty Isaf (13)

Neolithic long barrow
Location: Near Pengenfford, some 7km south of Talgarth
(SO 181 290)
Access: On private land, but permission to visit may
be gained from Ty Isaf Farm

One of the more carefully excavated tombs in Wales, Ty Isaf is located in a small valley between the two market towns of Talgarth and Crickhowell. From Talgarth, take the A497 south for approximately 7km to the hamlet of Pengenfford. From here, take the second turning on the left signposted 'Cwmfforest'. About 300m from this turning is Ty Isaf Farm where permission is required to visit the site. The long barrow lies on a small east-facing ridge in a field above the farm.

Ty Isaf was excavated in 1938 and is regarded as a 'hybrid' form of the Severn-Cotswold classification. Typically, it has a complex series of chambers and passages as well as a trapezoidal plan (oriented north/south), a false doorway and extended horns and façade. Although complex in plan, all that remains visually of this monument today are a few protruding orthostats and the remnants of the elongated mound (30m x 18m). However, the landscape setting can be regarded as an important element of the overall 'meaning' to its location and structure.

The plan reveals that Ty Isaf is a multi-phased monument, possibly with at least three phases of construction and use. Phase I consisted of a small oval cairn structure which is located at the southern end of the mound, and measures about 12m in diameter. Within the oval cairn is a south-east facing passage and a south-west/north-east oriented chamber. It has been argued that this structure was an addition to the larger mound plan (Corcoran 1969), but it is probable that it is the earliest structure, the larger trapezoidal mound being a later addition (Castleden 1992). Phase II, the main mound structure, has two chambers (with passages), and a curious false doorway. The mound itself is constructed of a double drystone revetment wall, with a doorway located at the northern end, between two horns. The plan and orientation is very similar to Pipton Long Barrow. Both the west and east lateral passages look out towards dominant topographic features: Mynydd Troed to the west and Waun Fach to the east. Approximately 100m to the west is the southward-flowing Afon Rhiangoll. It is the authors' view that these landscape features can be regarded as vital and necessary symbolic components of the overall plan, shape and location of Ty Isaf.

When excavated, Ty Isaf revealed a wealth of information about interring the dead. It would appear that all chambers and passages

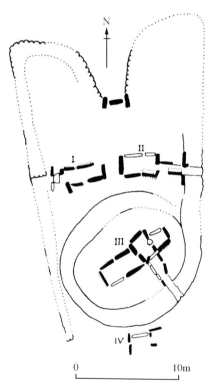

Ty Isaf (after Grimes)

0   10m

60

were utilised for disposing of the dead, but in different ways. In total, the remains of no fewer than 33 individuals were recovered. In the west chamber, crushed bones from 17 individuals, along with leaf-shaped arrowheads, a polished stone axe and undecorated Neolithic pottery were found. In the east chamber, one complete(?) skeleton was found along with six or more Western (Neolithic) bowls. Within the passage area, the remains of two articulated skeletons were also recovered, whilst outside, within the entrance area, a sandstone pendant and more pottery was found. Incidentally, pottery was also recovered from the old land surface against a section of the eastern wall (Daniel 1950). From the chamber and passage of the southern circular cairn more human remains were recovered; two articulated skeletons from the passage area and broken bones from the chamber plus a small quantity of undecorated Neolithic pottery. Phase III, a small isolated chamber at the southern end contained a Middle Bronze Age cremation urn and a series of burnt boxes which presumably once contained some of the remains.

The phases of construction plus the different ways in which the dead were interred suggests that Ty Isaf was in use over many hundreds of years, and certainly throughout the latter part of the Neolithic and Early Bronze Age. The small number of burials suggests either that bone material in some parts of the monument has not survived or, more likely, that it was only reserved for special individuals.

Mynydd Troed (14)

Neolithic long barrow
Location: 12km north-west of Crickhowell, on the flanks of
Mynydd Troed (SO 161 284)
Access: Can be easily reached from a nearby parking place

From Crickhowell, proceed north-west along the A40 to the A479. Approximately 9km along the A479, turn left onto a small narrow lane just before the hamlet of Pont Waun-fach. Proceed up this lane for about 3.7km. The Mynydd Troed oval cairn is located on a small rise about 30m from the lane and a small parking place.

Mynydd Troed, one of the Black Mountains Group's less impressive mounds lies 350m above sea level at the foot of Mynydd Troed and Llangorse Lake. The mound, oval (RCAHM[W] 1997 suggests 'quadrangular') in shape is oriented north-east/south-west and encloses a probable simple terminal chamber with at least one other chamber present. This monument, as with all others in this group, follows no group alignment. However, it is locally oriented to particular landscape features. The mound measures approximately 26.5m long and 15m at its widest point and stands around 1.5m high. The recent historical disturbance to this monument makes any reconstruction near impossible.

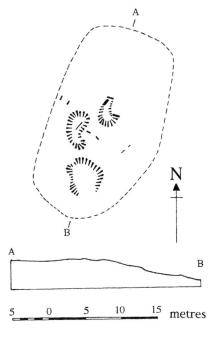

Mynydd Troed, plan and cross-section

However, Mynydd Troed does resemble other monuments within the group, in particular Penywyrlod, Ffostyll North and Ty Illtyd.

The site was discovered by O.G.S. Crawford in 1921 and sketched by Grimes in 1926. The sketch revealed possibly three orthostats and three exposed stone faces located centrally within the mound. There was also extensive disturbance within the southern section of the mound. In 1966 (Crampton & Webley), a series of sections were cut in the west and eastern sides of the mound in order to locate any possible walling, as well as taking environmental samples including pollen analysis of the site. According to RCAHM(W) (1997) excavation has identified the remains of an 11m long perimeter drystone wall approximately 0.43m high consisting of 22 thin courses. It appears that the walling had collapsed on the western side, but was protected by 'a canted pile of slabs' on the east (*ibid*. 35). Similar drystone walling is recorded during the excavations at Gwernvale. The excavation produced cherty flint flakes and various types of Neolithic pottery which are similar to artefacts found at Ty Isaf. The authors have noted there are at least three substantial hollows within the mound structure which possibly locate the position of three former chambers. Within two of these hollows are the tops of a number of upright stones. Past interpretation of the monument suggests that the stone alignments within the mound core indicate that Mynydd Troed has a terminal-chamber. However, we would argue that the stone alignments represent a possible western passage leading to a central chamber. Due to denudation of the monument, in particular within the northern section, there may have been further passages and chambers which rival the complexity of nearby Ty Isaf. Very little has been said about this monument due in part to its poor state of preservation.

Mynydd Troed has one of the more impressive landscape settings of all the Black Mountains Group. It is located between Mynydd Troed and Mynydd Llangors and faces south-east towards Cwm Sorgwm and Pen Allt-mawr, the Mynydd Troed tomb also commands views westwards towards Llyn Llangors. Both Mynydd Troed and Ty Illtyd are equidistant from Llyn Llangors (approximately 3.5km) and therefore may be linked territorially.

Grimes (1936a) suggests that the area around the mound marks the boundary between open scrub and woodland. This being the case, very little would be intervisible with Mynydd Troed despite the fact that it is 350m above sea level. The authors share the view that this tomb is sited in order to be seen, and argue that a large area of bracken-scrub and woodland would have been cleared in order to expose the mound to the surrounding landscape and recleared over time.

Penywyrlod (15)

Neolithic long barrow
Location: 2.5km south-west of Talgarth (150 315)
Access: On private land but permission may be gained
from the farm

This monument lies on a small rise overlooking Mynydd Troed. From Talgarth, head south for approximately 2km along the A479 towards Crickhowell. Take the first right signposted 'Penywyrlod Farm'. The farm is about 300m up this narrow lane. From the farm, walk due west through two fields, and Penywyrlod long barrow can be clearly seen on a small ridge. A barbed wire fence (with stile at the north end) surrounds the monument. Permission is required from Penywyrlod Farm before visiting this monument.

Excavated in 1972, Penywyrlod (not to be confused with Pen-y-Wyrlod, Llanigon), partially disguised by tree cover, was discovered through quarrying, the stone being used as hardcore. However, much of the chamber and passage plan at the southern end of the mound remain intact. The mound, one of the largest among the Black Mountains group, is of the 'hybrid' type synonymous with that of the later designs of the Severn-Cotswold group of monuments. Originally, Penywyrlod would have possessed two extended horns and a false portal at the southern end. However, these are not visible. Clearly present though are three chambers with disturbed capstones and the remains of two passages. Both chambers and passages look out towards the Black Mountains even though, to the west, the Brecon Beacons are also in full view. It would appear that the internal architecture is concerned only with the Black Mountains.

Situated 260m above sea level on the crest of a ridge above the Afon Llynfi Valley, this monument is clearly valley aligned, even though the orientation points blatantly towards Mynydd Troed. Also worth considering is the intervisibility with three other nearby tombs—Ffostyll North and South, and Pipton. All appear to be of similar architectural form, as well as having close affinities in various aspects of landscape topography and valley alignment.

The quarrying had destroyed a side chamber, exposed another on the north-eastern side and revealed the main architectural features of a false portal and centrally-positioned chamber lying beyond the main axis. Also revealed was the original outline of the mound which included substantial revetment walling on the north-eastern end of the mound and on the south-eastern 'horn' within the forecourt area. Excavations at both ends of the axis suggests that the mound was originally 52m long x 22.5m wide. A total of six excavations took place, located mainly on the north-eastern-facing revetment wall and exposed three side chambers, a central chamber and north-eastern 'horn'. The central chamber, possibly entered from the north-eastern side, revealed two orthostats (still visible today). Between these was an attempt to deliberately infill with earth and sandstone blocking. Britnell and Savory's report of 1972 suggests the orthostats were tilted inwards in order to support a large capstone(s). The whole structure was then covered by a rubble cairn. The north-eastern chamber had been almost totally destroyed, all that remained being a single orthostat which appeared to be defining two separate compartments measuring 2m x 1.2m and 1.6m x 1m. The latter compartment was entered from a passage between two revetment walls. The second chamber, located on the north-eastern side, consisted of a series of fallen uprights and

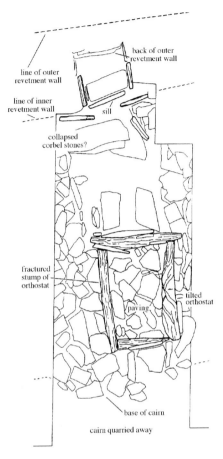

line of outer revetment wall

back of outer revetment wall

line of inner revetment wall

sill

collapsed corbel stones?

fractured stump of orthostat

tilted orthostat

paving

base of cairn

cairn quarried away

The Lateral Chamber NE 1

measured 2.85m x 1m x 1.3m high. This chamber was sealed by a slab and resembled a false entrance, similar to other chamber entrances within the Severn-Cotswold group. The third and final chamber excavated, located at the terminal end of the mound, included an entrance with supporting revetment walls.

A substantial quantity of disarticulated human bone was recovered from chambers 2 and 3. Within chamber 2, long bones were piled against the foot of the side walls. Adjoining chamber 3, human remains were discovered from the chamber's external area which according the RCAHM(W) (1997) may form part of an ossuary deposit. Along with human remains was a flint knife, a possible bone flute and a large selection of animal bones. Within the same chamber area, beneath the entrance, were several fragments of Abingdon ware. This ware, dated between 2500 and 3000 bc, is usually characterised by a thick rolled rim which is decorated with oblique incisions, twisted cord impressions and multiple rows of circular stabs and oblique incisions (Gibson 1986:16).

Ty Illtyd (16)

Neolithic long barrow
Location: Near Llanhamlach, 3km south-east of Brecon
(SO 098 263)
Access: On private land but permission may be gained
from the farm

From the roundabout at the eastern end of the Brecon by-pass, head along the A40 towards Crickhowell. Approximately 2km along this road and past the village of Llanhamlach, turn left on a small narrow country lane signposted 'Pennorth'. About 700m up this lane is Manest Court Farm, where permission is required in order to visit the site. Opposite the farm and located approximately 800m away on an east-facing ridge is Ty Illtyd (also known as Ty Illtud and Maen Iltyd).

Ty Illtyd, although classified within the Black Mountains Group, is the only tomb that is divorced from the main group and has a landscape affinity with the Brecon Beacons. Situated on a west-facing ridge, 320m OD and approximately 6.6km due west of Mynydd Troed, Ty Illtyd overlooks the flood plains of the river Usk and incorporates the whole of the eastern extent of the Brecon Beacons. Both the chamber and the capstone are aligned towards Pen y Fan, the highest point within the Brecon Beacons. This site was first investigated by John Aubrey in the 17th century and later by Edward Lhuyd in 1695, who described the monument as having three uprights and one capstone with clear graffiti on both side stones (leading to the chamber). He also noted that the chamber was encased in a circular mound. Since then the site has been subjected to intensive ploughing resulting in possible kerbing being uprooted and destroyed.

The monument is constructed of a single capstone overlying a rectangular chamber, delineated by eight uprights and set into a raised oval earthen mound measuring 23m (north/south) x 15.7m (east/west). The mound slopes to the south and west and the chamber, measuring 1m x 2m, is oriented north/south with a small rectangular forecourt or antechamber at the northern end, which Corcoran (1969) suggested may be a second chamber. The RCAHM(W) report (1997) confuses the reader with endless dimensions. However, in most cases, a picture is worth a thousand words and Henry Longueville Jones' 1867 engraving is no exception (see p.34). The drawing clearly shows a series of uprights and a capstone, which opens out to the north-north-east and clearly defines a possible forecourt opening. The two outer uprights depicted in the engraving may represent the inner sections of two horns.

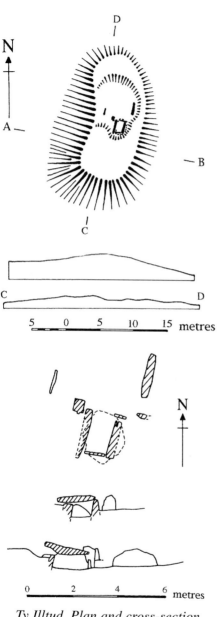

On five of the uprights is a series of medieval-type inscriptions (probable graffiti). The faded rock art includes a harp (five-stringed lyre) and two dates of 1312 (in Roman numerals) and 1510. One of the side chamber uprights bears at least eight cross inscriptions and what are presumed to be personal initials. The other side upright has at least 60 symbols, the majority being lozenges, diamonds and crosses (see opposite). Longueville Jones (*Arch. Camb.* 22, 1867:347-55) considered them to be the work of 'shepherd boys'. The Abbé Breuil (1935:290) and O.G.S. Crawford (1925: 156) have argued that the origin of some of the graffiti is prehistoric, if not contemporary with the use of the tomb. On the other hand Leslie Grinsell (1981:131-9) considered that the tomb had been reused during the Christian period as a hermit's cell belonging to St Illtyd, and that the symbols are of medieval

Ty Illtud. Plan and cross-section (above), and plan and section of chamber (below)

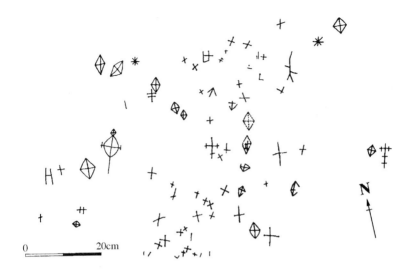

Ty Illtud, medieval inscription from the orthostats
(*from* Archaeologia Cambrensis *1981*)

date, whilst the The RCAHM(W) report (1997) has stated that the early dates are unlikely as the graffiti has close associations with masons' marks contemporary with the robbing of the monument for building stone. We would add that the marks, as illustrated in *Archaeologia Cambrensis* (1981), are not prehistoric, for there are no direct parallels with prehistoric art elsewhere, but we would also add that this is not idle graffiti. If the crosses are Christian they may represent a refuge against persecution similar to incised art found in the Cathar region of south-western France.

Gwernvale (17)

Neolithic long barrow
Location: 1.5km north-west of Crickhowell (SO 211 192)
Access: Adjacent to the A40

Gwernvale, one of the so-called 'hybrid' Severn-Cotswold monuments, is located alongside the A40. The central chamber can be clearly seen from the road, close to the entrance of the Gwernvale Manor Hotel. In the recent past, damage has occurred to one of the side chamber orthostats.

Excavated many times in the past, the last time in 1977-78 by Britnell and Savory, Gwernvale is sited on an earlier Neolithic settlement. Evidence also suggests that flint from the Late Upper Palaeolithic (*c*.12,000 BC) is also present. According to Burnham (1995:15), intensive early farming activity was present on the site, dating to 3900 BC. Here were discovered pits, associated pottery and the remains of two rectangular buildings. The buildings, identified by two rows of six post holes within the forecourt area and beneath the northern horn, were aligned in the same direction as the later cairn. The elongated mound, constructed of a double revetment wall, is oriented east/west. Britnell (1979) noted traces of a possible ancient cement between the uprights and drystone walling during the 1977-78 excavation.

Gwernvale aroused some early interest from the Breconshire historian Theophilus Jones, who in 1809, remarked: 'This cromlech, one end of which adjoined the Brecon turnpike road on the south side, was immediately opposite Gwernvale, about half-a-mile from Crickhowell: it consisted as usual of a huge tablet of unhewn stone mounted upon five supporters pitched edgewise in the ground, the super incumbent stone or cover inclining to the south and open in the front to the north; it was placed on a high mound, long overrun with brushwood and brambles, and formerly there seem to have been stones placed edgewise also round what is now almost a semicircle; whether before the turnpike road was made they extended it so as to describe an irregular circle I know not; but I am inclined to think that the appearance of the spot was materially altered by the intersection of the highway; and that upon that occasion the workmen ... anticipated our attempt to make discoveries under the cromlech; in that case the object, though far different from ours, was probably equally unsuccessful. ... The experiment in

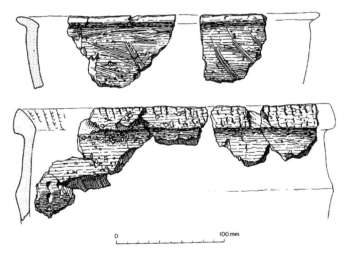

Pottery from Gwernvale. Top: plain round-bottomed bowl;
Lower: decorated Peterborough bowl
(from Britnell and Savory 1984)

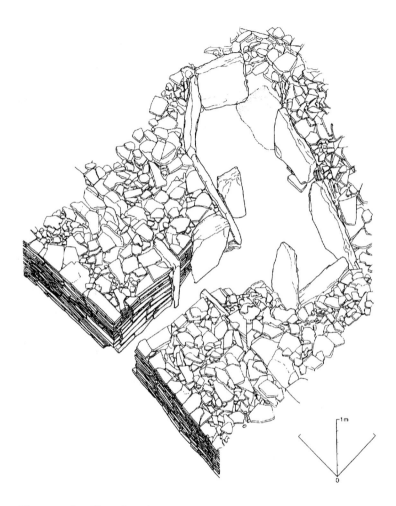

Gwernvale. Chamber 3, axonometric projection showing drystone walling and chamber uprights (from Britnell and Savory 1984)

1804 proved nothing either way (as to the sepulchral or other object of the cromlech).'

A quite different account from the unpublished diary of Sir Richard Colt Hoare states: 'Saturday May 26th 1803. This morning was devoted to opening a cromlech or kistvaen adjoining the turn-pike road near Crickhowell and opposite the house of Mr Everett: with some difficulty the upper stone measuring ten feet in length, being removed, we dug to the base of the surrounding upright stones, which had supported the recumbent one, but found no signs of an interment or relics; but a few pieces of charcoal seemed to indicate cremation. The history of the cromlech has not as yet been sufficiently ascertained, and it remains a doubt whether it was designed for an altar or sepulchre. The kistvaen or stone chest was clearly designed for an interment.' O.G.S. Crawford (1925:60) noticed the chamber was being used as 'a receptacle for old pails, bottles and jam jars'.

Forty-five metres in length and standing on a low sandy gravel terrace, the mound was once thought to be circular in form (Fenton 1804, Crawford 1925). At the eastern end are two horns and a false portal. Two lateral chambers are located at the southern end of the mound, both are clearly visible (see illustration p.37). The largest chamber, polygonal in shape, comprises six large uprights and has a passage that opens out towards dominant topographic features—the River Usk and Mynydd Llangatwg in the south-west. A third chamber also exists but has been badly damaged along with a small single chamber on the northern side. Very little in the way of human remains were found during the 1978 excavation. However, it is believed that human remains were removed in 1804.

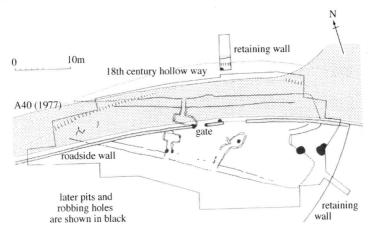

Gwernvale showing its position in relation to the A40
(from Britnell and Savory 1984)

Garn Goch (18)

Neolithic long barrow
Location: In Ffawyddog, south of Crickhowell (SO 212 177)
Access: In public play area

Garn Goch (also referred to as Carn Goch) lies within the village of Ffawyddog, close to the River Usk. This monument is a 'hybrid' Severn-Cotswold tomb, similar to Gwernvale. From Crickhowell head south across the Usk to a T-junction. Turn left onto the A4077 and take the first right signposted 'Ffawyddog'. Approximately 300m along this road take the first left to a small housing estate and children's play area. Garn Goch lies within the play area.

Garn Goch lies on a small rise, 85m OD, overlooking the

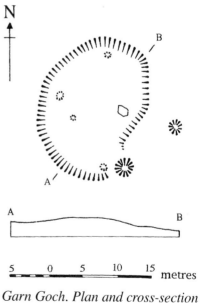

Garn Goch. Plan and cross-section

76

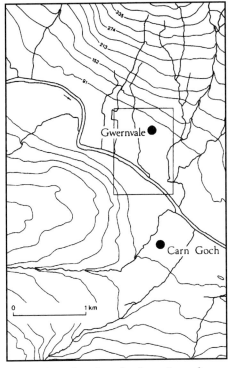

Map showing the location of Gwernvale and Garn Goch on either side of the river Usk (from Britnell and Savory 1984)

river Usk and with views towards the surrounding mountains to the north and south. The monument was discovered accidentally in 1847 by workmen clearing stones from Llangattock Park. According to an anonymous account in *Archaeologia Cambrensis* (1854:148) when found the mound had housed a 'cist' or 'cromlech' which was supported by four 'rude uprights' under a covering stone. Human remains were found, some of which 'crumbled to dust' according to a report in the *Gentleman's Magazine* of 1847. However, a humerus and maxilla (upper jaw) with a row of teeth and part of a skull were retained intact. It appears that the bones were housed within a chamber measuring 2.6m x 1.22m x 0.7m high. Accompanying the bones was a 'quantity of fresh-looking charcoal'.

The form of this monument is very difficult to decipher. However, Crawford, visiting with Mortimer Wheeler in 1924, suggested it was a long cairn and 'typical of other Breconshire examples'. The mound, which measures 17.4m in diameter and is 1.6m high, is oval-shaped with its northern end oriented towards Table Mountain, a prominent truncated spur on the southern edge of the Black Mountains. In the recent past, the mound has been subjected to disturbance from tree roots and possible 'vandalism'. On the north side of the mound, where the chamber was found, there is at present a large capstone slab measuring 1.6m x 1.5m lying over the chamber. Both Crawford (1925) and Grimes (1936a) suggested that Garn Goch was indeed a long cairn, possibly similar in form to nearby Gwernvale. Daniel (1950), however, argued that it was no more than a cist or round mound. We tend to agree with Crawford and Grimes. Although the mound is presently oval in shape, its original form may be typical of other megalithic structures in the region. There are a number of large stones 'placed' on top of the mound and delineating a simple rectangular chambered structure. Finally, many of the landscape 'traits' attributed to the monuments in this region such as topographic orientation also apply to Garn Goch.

The Bronze Age

Still Locked in Stone: The Neolithic/Bronze Age transition

A shift from corporate monumentality to single-status cairns and round barrows indicates that, around 2500 BC, profound social changes were taking place. Unlike the large Neolithic monuments that occupy intermediate slopes and occasionally river valleys, cairns (which can be divided into round cairns with cist, structured cairns, ring cairns, kerb cairns and barrow cemeteries) are found high on the tops of hills and mountains as well as in valley locations. There are approximately 1,600 of these monuments in Breconshire.

This change in landscape position coincides with a possible rise in population (Burnham 1995:18). Some argue that rough figures for this may be calculated by multiplying the number of barrows by a factor of three (the average number of individuals interred within each monument) (Atkinson 1972:114), assuming that all of the population were buried in barrows. However, we would stress that this was not the case and that only high status individuals were so buried, making this equation heavily flawed and the population figure probably much higher. Even so, the re-organisation of the landscape may have had more to do with the emergence of social élites and consolidation of social and political territories rather than population dynamics. Highly visible on the skyline, cairns may be seen as statements of land ownership that, over time, increased in symbolic value owing to their association with ancestors. Nearly every hill, mountain peak and valley appears to have a cairn or round barrow, so it is difficult to recognise territorial groups. The RCAHM(W) inventory (1997:73) suggests that there is no general pattern for cairn location.

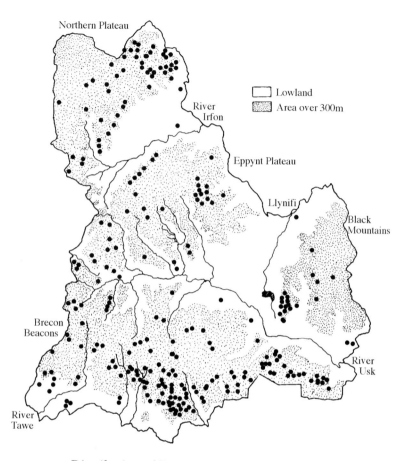

Distribution of Bronze Age burial monuments

Other monuments and symbolic earthworks dating from this transitional period include henges, cursus monuments, stone circles and, in this part of Wales, stone rows. The basis of a ritual landscape are the more permanent landscape markers such as stone circles, henges and barrows. In the case of the Walton Basin and Welshpool valley, in neighbouring Radnorshire, there is the added monumentality of a series of cursus monuments and a large circular enclosure. Although not directly associated with burial, these may form part of the burial complex and some have identified the emergence of local traditions (Burnham 1995:19). Single standing stones were favoured in north-eastern Clwyd, for example, while to the west and south, groups of cairns with a variety of characteristics prevailed. The same is true of stone circles. These are rare in Clwyd but well established in Powys, where they form a number of clusters. In neither area is it likely that we are seeing the full story, for many Welsh Neolithic monuments were damaged as part of a rise in Celtic superstition and vandalism over the last three centuries (Daniel 1950; Powell *et al* 1969) and many of the more insignificant monuments of the Bronze Age probably met a similar fate. We can agree with the idea of monument clusters but we would stress that other monuments such as timber and earthen structures add to a landscape package that is both dynamic and fluid through time. By this we mean that single monuments such as standing stones or stone rows fall in and out of ritual use and that unlike the Neolithic, the set standard disposing of the dead throughout the Bronze Age was cremation, initially using beakers and later urns—large decorated and undecorated vessels. These usually ended up buried within the thin soils beneath cairns and, in a few cases, under barrows. Further east, across the Herefordshire border, there is evidence of urn cemeteries without cairn or barrow (Children & Nash:1994). As in the succeeding Iron Age, associated settlements occupy conspicuous locations, such as the plateaus and hinterlands of the Cambrian Mountains. Enclosures usually consist of stone-lined hut circles arranged in clusters of three or four. Remains tend to survive well in the uplands, simply because they have been ignored by farmers, but it is a different story in the rich fertile valleys of the Usk, Wye and Severn. The settlement pattern may have been similar to that found in alpine regions, with upland grazing and some crop agriculture during the summer months, while winters were spent in the protective surrounds of the valleys.

With regard to settlement in the Bronze Age and perhaps the early Iron Age, it is necessary to consider the enigmatic phenomenon of the burnt mound. These mounds usually comprise a small depression or pit which, when excavated, is normally defined as a rectangular stone-lined feature which would have held water. Close to this feature is a series of burnt stones. Archaeologists have interpreted both the stones and the feature as being associated with cooking, suggesting that the stones were heated on a fire and placed into water in the rectangular structure in which meat would also have been placed. There are approximately 20 such sites in Breconshire; more have been discovered in south-west Wales and Ireland. The Royal Commission (1997:184) refers to these mounds as 'boiling mounds' or 'prehistoric hearths'. We would suggest, however, that they represent something more symbolic, in that they may have functioned as baths or cleansing sites (Barfield & Hodder 1987:370-379).

It was not until around 2100 BC that bronze began being manufactured in the British Isles. This development marks the end of the long transitional period between the Late Neolithic and the Bronze Age proper during which copper artefacts appeared. The European Copper Age commenced around 4500 BC (3700 bc) (Parker-Pearson 1993:17) but does not really begin in Britain until 2500 BC. The smelting and casting of copper and bronze implements was only possible following technological innovation. This involved using small open bowl furnaces, fuelled by charcoal to achieve the extremely high temperatures needed to melt copper ore (1,083 degrees centigrade) through the use of bellows. Impurities were then removed from the molten metal cake which was then reheated in a crucible (made from heat-resistant clay) until it liquefied. The molten metal was then poured into clay/stone moulds. The influences giving rise to copper technology are of Continental origin, with Middle/Late Neolithic dates for copper production recorded for central Europe. The recently-discovered 'Ice Man',

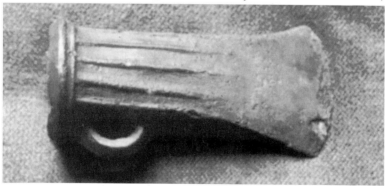

Late Bronze Age single-looped socketed axe
(from Brecknock Museum)

Selection of late Bronze Age metal artefacts including a spear-head (from Hay-on-Wye), a palstave (from Ffynhonnan, Brecon) and a socketed axe (from Bronllys) held in Brecknock Museum

who perished in the Italian/Austrian Alps, carried with him an axe made from copper which was dated to the early Neolithic (*c*.4000 BC). In Britain, this phase is referred to as the 'Beaker Period', named after a distinctive decorated vessel which may have served a number of uses, but usually ended up in burials. The 'Beaker' burial package also included cremation, a trait which is evident during the Late Neolithic, with remains being interred in food vessels (of the Collared-Rim tradition) and placed beneath round barrows and cairns. (Collared urns, usually decorative in appearance, derive, according to Gibson (1986) from late Neolithic Peterborough ware. The most discernable features are the rim and the collar.) Also present are copper daggers, jet buttons and copper archers' wrist guards. Alas, these are quite rare (Savory 1980b).

How did such artefacts, which originated in central Europe and the Low Countries, arrive in Wales? Migration is the traditional solution to this question, skilled metal-workers forming part of an influx of people into Britain at this time (Burnham 1995:18). The theory, which seems 'to fit the facts at present known', plays down the role of local cultural change in favour of external influences, either in the form of a single migratory episode or a series of waves

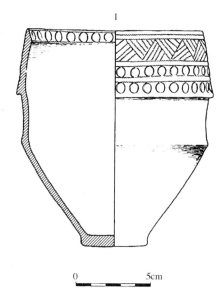

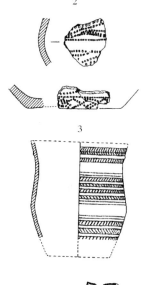

1. *Middle to Late Bronze Age Cinerary Urn of the Collared-rim type from a cist at Llangynidr (Savory 1980)*
2. *Early Bronze Age Beaker base fragment with notched chevron and lozenge patterning from the Neolithic tomb of Ty Isaf (Savory 1980)*
3. *Early to Middle Bronze Age Beaker with notched decoration from Penderyn (Savory 1980)*
4. *Early Bronze Age Beaker base fragment with notched linear decoration from Cwm Cadlan, Penderyn (Savory 1980)*
5. *Middle to Late Bronze Age Pygmy cup with a herringbone type corded decoration from Llanfihangel Cwm-du (Savory 1980)*

(Savory 1980a:15). However, it does not have to be people who move, merely ideas and these could be transmitted as part of prestige exchanges between élites on both sides of the Channel. Eventually, the ideas associated with the Early Bronze Age cultural package would have trickled into Wales. This was why there is such an immense time span between the end of the Neolithic and the beginning of the Bronze Age proper.

This lengthy transitional period, from people working with stone tools to working with bronze, exceeds 500 years. The question must arise therefore, is the Early Bronze Age actually a bronze age? Copper technology, one of the main elements of bronze, appears to have reached Britain by about 2400 BC (Burnham 1995:18). This technological innovation appears as part of a complex package of ideas concerning status, prestige and burial, the items themselves appearing to be linked with monuments associated with burial and ritual. The earthen bank monuments of the Late Neolithic and Early Bronze Age—henges and cursus monuments—together with stone circles, standing stones and stone rows appear to pass out of use around 1600 BC, although the evidence suggests that the more obvious visible stone monuments were, in fact, used as territorial markers for preceding upland societies during the Bronze Age.

The Means of Production: Metal in the Bronze Age
It is difficult to pinpoint precisely where one period ends and another begins. Archaeologists have tended to rely solely upon changes in artefacts and monuments. Savory (1980b:16), for example, subdivides the Early Bronze Age (EBA) into EBA I (*c*.2500 - 2000 BC), EBA II (*c*.2000 -1750 BC) and EBA III (*c*.1750-1450 BC). The MBA (*c*.1450-900 BC) is also subdivided into three phases: MBA I (*c*.1450-1250 BC), MBA II (*c*.1250-1050 BC) and MBA III (*c*.1050-900 BC). Each of these is named after a type site: MBA I (Acton Park, Denbighshire), MBA II (Cemmaes, Montgomeryshire) and MBA III (Penard, Glamorgan). All three have revealed distinct Welsh bronze implement hoards. Savory's Later Bronze Age (*c*.900-600 BC) is characterised by the growth of regional metalworking and the consolidation of territories. Interestingly, other archaeologists such as Darvill (1987) place the transition between the Bronze Age and the Iron Age at around 900 BC.

A number of general trends are apparent from around 2300 BC, when copper began to be superseded by the more versatile bronze, an alloy of copper and tin that was used to produce flat axes and, by 1700 BC, the distinctive palstave tool/weapon (see overleaf).

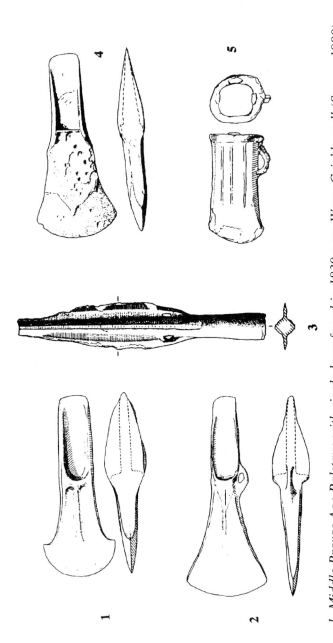

1. Middle Bronze Age Palstave with single loop found in 1839 near Wern, Crickhowell (Savory 1980)
2. Middle Bronze Age Palstave with single loop found during reservoir construction at Vaynor (Savory 1980)
3. Late Bronze Age double looped spearhead found in the River Wye near Hay-on-Wye (Savory 1980)
4. Middle to Late Bronze Age Haft-flanged Axe found under peat at Llanbedr Ystradwy (Savory 1980)
5. Late Bronze Age single looped Socketed Axe found at Pant-y-wenalt farm, Llandetty (Savory 1980)

Although largely standardised in shape and size, these tools did evolve regional forms. A project undertaken by the Board of Celtic Studies grouped 550 bronze artefacts according to composition (Northover 1980:229). The earliest Welsh metal was an 'impure copper' which had been alloyed with arsenic (*ibid*. 235), later tin bronze consisted of 10-12 per cent tin and emerged during the latter part of the Early Bronze Age. This phase was dominated by ceramics and saw the disappearance of beakers and inhumation burials and the use of cinerary urns (food vessels with collared rims) and 'pygmy cups'. Introducing lead to the alloy (between two and seven per cent) improved 'casting behaviour', owing to a much lower melting point, and facilitated production of the more ornate moulded implements of the Middle Bronze Age, a period coinciding with the rapid disappearance of fine lithics. By increasing the tin content to 15 per cent, harder and more durable implements could be cast, but at higher temperatures. Achieving the optimum blend of constituents for each artefact type would have required much experimentation.

In Breconshire, a number of gold items have been recovered, in addition to the usual array of bronze tools, suggesting not only the existence of high-ranking individuals, but also technical innovation and superior craftsmanship on the part of local smiths as they and metalworkers to the north applied their skills to the task of shaping the area's prosperity. Further innovation followed in the form of the versatile socketed axe, which was manufactured using a two-piece mould. Swords, spearheads and domestic implements are also much in evidence. However, not all finds should be attributed to local producers. The presence of regional characteristics suggests exchanges were taking place with other core areas outside central Wales, possibly coinciding with later Iron Age tribal domains. Socketed axes may have arrived in the area from as far afield as South Wales (Burnham 1995:21).

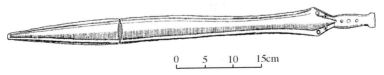

0   5   10   15cm

A Late Bronze Age Ewart type Bronze sword from Cwm-du found
by John Thomas Powell (Savory 1980)

Some of the single looped socketed axes that formed part of a hoard found at Penwyllt, Ystradgynlais (Savory 1980)

Towards the end of the Middle Bronze Age, a sharp climatic downturn brought cooler, wetter conditions, the consequences of which appear to have been quite dramatic. Beset by heavy rainfall and colder winters, and contending with soils which, after more than 400 years of continuous use, had become worked out and exhausted, people deserted the uplands of central Wales in favour of the more fertile coastal areas and river valleys. Gradually, through a combination of causes including climatic deterioration, the whole of Middle Bronze Age Europe sank into social, political and economic turmoil. The early Greek civilisation of Mycenae collapsed. In Britain, many 'public monuments' appear to have fallen into disuse (Burnham 1995:21), while pits and bogs swallowed up deposits of metalwork, including gold. Some of the hoards found have included flat axes, socketed axes, palstaves and daggers such as the Late Bronze Age hoard at Penwyllt near Ystradgynlais. At this site a number of single looped socketed axes (see drawing above), tanged chisels and a sword blade were found just below the ground surface, near a large boulder on a mountain above Penwyllt (Savory 1980:122). Others have contained scrap pieces which may have been intended for re-use after recovery.

Stone Signatures on the Landscape

Monuments such as stone settings and stone circles flourished throughout western Britain from 2500-1800 BC, the transitional period between the Late Neolithic and the emerging Early Bronze Age. These monuments, which are scattered throughout the landscape of Breconshire, do not readily reveal their function. Single stones may represent territorial markers or they may have had some kind of association with other monuments, such as cairns, which are abundant, or stone circles, of which there are few in this part of Wales. Multiple Bronze Age monument clusters are not only confined to Breconshire. A recent study incorporating Neolithic and Early Bronze Age monumentality around the Preseli Mountains in south-west Wales has also identified similar monument distribution (Children & Nash, 1996 & 1997). Within this research a number of criteria became apparent especially when looking at monument type and spatial distribution. Firstly, it was rare to find monuments individually sited within the landscape, Bronze Age barrows and cairns usually occurring in groups. Secondly, these groups were often associated either with standing stones or, in some cases, stone circles and stone rows—what we refer to as a 'total Bronze Age Landscape' (*ibid.* 32). The landscape of the Preseli Mountains can be organised into three zones; upland mountain, upland plateau and, to the south, undulating lowland pasture, a similar landscape to Breconshire. The majority of the Preseli monuments are located within the mountain and plateau zones, monument groups usually consisting of cairns (or tumuli), standing stones, and a single stone circle. Dispersed throughout the locality are a number of settlements which may relate to the symbolic monuments. We suggested that the siting of these monuments is deliberate and appears to 'act' as a series of doorways or processional markers leading from the plateau zone into an inner sacred landscape—that of the mountain zone. The starting point may be the stone circle, from which one is drawn through the landscape via a series of strategically placed standing stones, eventually leading to the cairns—the final resting place for the dead.

The Brecon Beacons National Park contains seven circles, of various shapes and sizes, within its bounds (Dorling 1996:5), five of which are found within a 20km area west of Brecon. One circle,

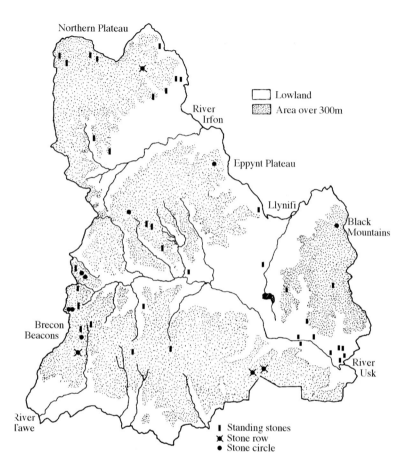

Distribution of Bronze Age symbolic monuments

that of Ynys-hir, is on land occupied by the Ministry of Defence and not able to be visited. Some claim that stone circles are aligned with specific phases of the rising and setting of the moon (prehistoric calendars or astrological observatories), the solstices and equinoxes 'providing a seasonal association of particular importance to the farming community' (Dorling *ibid.* 4). Above all, stone settings, stone circles, barrows and cairns emphasise the need for permanency. Collectively, they appear to create a statement within the landscape. These monuments, therefore, are not just markers but create and establish group identity.

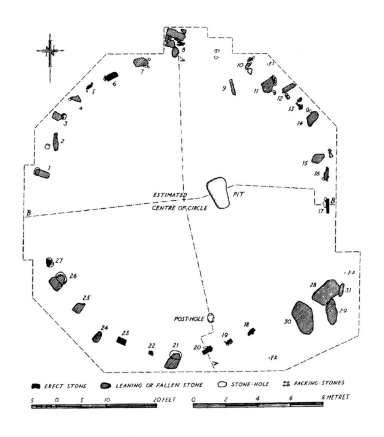

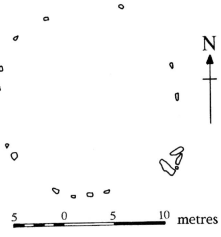

Above: Plan of the Ynys-hir stone circle (from G.C. Dunning, Arch. Camb. *97:1943)*

Left: As seen today.

The Dunning excavation revealed up to 31 stones whereas only 17 are visible today

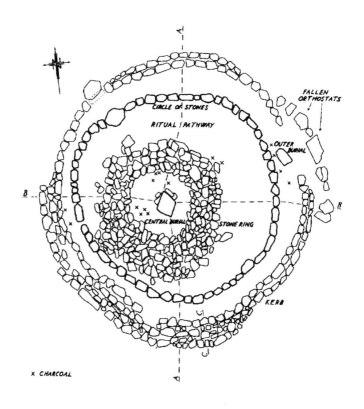

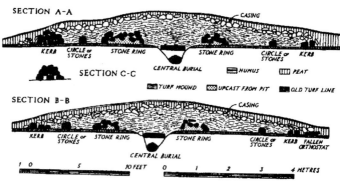

*Ynys-hir cairn (SN 921 383), plan and section
from* Archaeologia Cambrensis 97:1943)

The recently published RCAHM(W) report (1997) recognises 49 standing stones including eight which are now lost. However, we suggest that this number is very much underestimated, especially if one is to include the more than probable examples that lie recumbent close to a number of stone circles. The report, though, has listed a further 75 sites, which are either unexcavated or recently included within the inventory, but subsequently regards the unexcavated stones as natural erratics and rejects them. We have suggested that standing stones, along with stone circles, stone rows and cairns, form part of a multi-site complex. Moreover, they appear to be organised in such a way as to move people around the landscape (Children & Nash, 1997). Despite the statement by the RCAHM(W) that standing stones are an enigmatic group of monuments difficult to classify, we suggest that many of the stones within the county are indeed large enough and arranged in such a way with other monuments to suggest antiquity. Moreover, in the majority of cases this group of monuments appear in association with other Bronze Age monuments, thus reinforcing the notion of the 'complex'. With regard to dating genuine prehistoric standing stones, we take the view that if these stones are distributed in the vicinity of sites which are Bronze Age in date, it can be assumed that these too are contemporary. Very few artefacts have been found close to standing stones, but within the county and elsewhere a number of stones do possess definite cupmark designs which are invariably Bronze Age in date. This enigmatic group of monuments, by their nature literally individual stones sticking out of the ground, has warranted little interest in the past. Most of the standing stones have weathered surfaces, caused by the elements eroding the soft Old Red Sandstone, making the location of any cupmarks near impossible except in a few cases. A further problem is that of original location—many stones throughout Britain have, at one time or another, been re-erected during historical times in order to suit parish boundary or waymarker needs, or even to serve as cattle 'scratching' posts. Barber & Williams (1989:14) have suggested that standing stones dating from what he terms 'the Dark Age', may have possessed painted inscriptions or patterns. However, there are no traces of either on any of the stones in Breconshire. In the early 1940s Sir Cyril Fox excavated around the Maen Madoc standing stone, but failed to establish a definite date. The stone does have so-called 'Dark Age' inscriptions, but these could be inscribed on to a standing stone that dates to the Bronze Age. The excavation could also not ascertain with certainty its original position.

Earlier it has been shown that monuments do not appear in isolation. Neolithic chambered tombs form groups which usually possess unique architectural or landscape affinities. Certainly, within this part of Wales, standing stones, along with cairns, stone rows and stone circles appear to be inextricably linked. This phenomenon is certainly present with the upland monument groups around the Trecastle area. Another interesting anomaly which reinforces the notion that standing stones are processional or guiding markers are the eight or so standing stones that are strategically distributed along the lower reaches of the Usk Valley from Crickhowell to Brecon. The valley is flanked by two major massifs: to the south, the dominant ridges of Mynydd Llangynidr and Nangatwg, whilst to the north, the dramatic peaks of Pen Cerrig-calch and Mynydd Llangors overlook a fertile flood plain which contains not only Neolithic remains but a series of Bronze Age monuments. Within the valley there is a plateau on which are eight strategically placed standing stones and, to the north, a number of cairns located on the highest points. Between Brecon and Gilwern, in the south-east, are eight standing stones on the lower flood plains close to the river Usk. Standing stones are placed at strategic points either along the valleys of tributaries or else marking the mouths of smaller streams. The majority of these monuments, including the cairns, are found on the north side of the river. However, one standing stone and the Neolithic Garn Coch appear on the south side. To the north and east of Llangynidr, four standing stones surround a small hill known as the Myarth. They appear to be roughly equidistant from each other and seem to act as pathways or processional routes leading to the cairns on top of Pen Cerrig-calch, Pen Galch-y-pibwr and Mynydd Llangors. Similar paths have been identified on Grey Hill, near Caldicot, Monmouthshire (Children & Nash 1996). What is overwhelming within this example is the survival and location of the standing stone complex and its relationship with the nearby cairns to the north. It would appear that the Usk acts as a boundary and that religious significance is placed upon lands to the north.

Of the eight standing stones, the Cwrt y gollen standing stone is the largest at over 4m high. Constructed of Old Red Sandstone the monolith has a crescent-shaped notch a metre from the top of the eastern edge of the stone. This stone in its present position, and assuming that no other standing stones were located south-east along the Usk, marks the start or termination of a processional route along the Usk Valley towards Brecon. To the north-east of the Cwrt y gollen monument and within the village boundary of Llangenny are two further stones, one of which is Maen Llwyd on Pen y Gader Fawr. This stands 2.18m high and occupies one of the highest locations in the county. According to the RCAHM(W) report (1997), this monument is part of a field boundary. However, the authors visiting the site in early 1998, saw no evidence of any such boundary. What was evident was that the stone stood on a crescent ridge approximately 1.5m high—very similar to the standing stone at Bwlch, some 7km up the Usk Valley. Approximately 1.5km north of the Maen Llwyd stone, is the Druid's Altar Stone, which stands on the western bank of the Grwyne Fawr. The two Afon Grwyne Fawr stones appear to be isolated monuments; located in a discrete valley with no intervisibility. Assuming they are of prehistoric date, both monuments do arguably lead to cairns a few kilometres to the north.

Approximately 4km north-west up the Usk Valley and beyond the Gwernvale chambered tomb, is a series of four large standing

The standing stone at Bwlch

stones which occupy positions close to the Usk and its tributaries. All four stones also encircle a small hillock known as Myarth and, like all other stones within this area, occupy locations north of the river Usk—very few monuments of Bronze Age date are located south of the river. Beyond the standing stone at Bwlch, approximately 3km south, located on the flood plain, is the Llwyn y Fedwen standing stone which is made from erratic limestone. It stands 4.27m high and was erected on a small natural glacial mound (RCAHM[W] 1997) 60m long by 4m high. The stone itself leans slightly to the north and is reputedly among the tallest in Wales. During the 13th century the stone was probably used as a marker for tithe lands by the monks of Brecon. The final stone within this group, the Battle Stone, is in the village of Llanhamlach, near the chambered tomb of Ty Illtud and a Roman road. This blunt pointed Old Red Sandstone monolith stands 3.96m high and, again, is located on a glacial mound oriented north-south (10m x 0.9m). The RCAHM(W) report (1997) suggests that the mound may originally have been a cairn. With regards to the distribution of Bronze Age monuments beyond the Battle Stone, there are only a few isolated cairns farther west, around the western approaches of the Brecon Beacons. The next significant cluster, which includes mainly stone circles and stone rows, is located around Trecastell. The spatial distribution of these monuments is interesting inasmuch as most are located along the reaches and intermediate slopes of the Usk Valley. Strangely, there is very little evidence of monument-building on the Brecon Beacons, Mynydd Llangattock to the south, and the Black Mountains to the north.

Encroaching the Uplands: Environmental considerations

The Bronze Age is not only characterised by changes in material culture, but also by shifts in climate and other environmental changes. One of the best sources of evidence is a number of pollen sequences which have been taken from archaeological sites where peat is present. Although the resultant pollen diagrams for the Bronze Age (post-elm decline) lack accurate dates (Caseldine 1990:55), patterns do emerge, such as small-scale forest clearances followed by a burst of more intense activity. This regime probably represents the transitional period between the Late Neolithic and

Early Bronze Age. Clearances are recognised in pollen sequences at Pwll-nant-ddu in central Wales (Wiltshire and Moore 1983) and in others derived from a buried soil surface beneath a barrow at Penrhyncoch. Cereal pollen is also present at a number of sites. It therefore seems likely that a change from mixed farming to a more pastoral regime, together with increased cereal cultivation, coincided with the Beaker period, *c*.2500 BC. Towards the Middle Bronze Age, the uplands began to be utilised for pastoral farming and, in some parts, cereal cultivation. The effect would have been to place upland soils under great strain. At around the same time, a marked increase in rainfall resulted in upland mires and bogs and a series of well-stratified peat sequences, especially within central and west Wales. One of the major type sites where extensive pollen and macro-faunal work has been undertaken is Tregaron bog. A series of Bronze Age and Iron Age clearances have been dated, the latter to 2354 + 110 BP (reference no: Q-596) (Turner 1964). Caseldine (1990) has outlined an excellent synthesis of all the major environmental sites within Wales. Unfortunately, only a handful occur within Breconshire. Generally, the climate in this part of Wales was slightly cooler and wetter than during the Neolithic. Upland erosion of soils due to human agencies such as woodland clearance and cultivation regimes, saw a need to consolidate these marginal lands. It must be assumed that similar regimes existed elsewhere, with the exception of the coastal areas of North Wales (including Anglesey) and south-west Wales, where potential crop-growing is increased from 240 days to 365 days per year accommodating both spring and autumn planting and later harvesting (Fowler 1983:24). A peat sequence at Llanllwch, near Carmarthen, has revealed two phases of clearance before 1800 BC, but falling within the Early/Middle Bronze Age (Thomas 1965). A marked decline in lime (*tilia*) pollen followed by the appearance of cereal pollen indicates an upturn in agricultural activity around the beginning of the Middle Bronze Age. Roughly six phases of climatic deterioration have been noted at Tregaron between 4500-500 BP (Turner 1964), suggesting, overall, a gradual downturn towards a more maritime climate. At Waun-Fignen-Felin, further upland Bronze Age clearances have been recognised (Cloutman 1983 and Smith & Cloutman 1988). Here, a decline in lime coincides with that of elm. The date of this decline varies between *c.*4059 BP and *c.*3750 BP. Also present are the charred macro-fossil remains of upland herbs, possibly the result of deliberate heath-burning. Significant decreases in arboreal or tree pollen, coupled with rising values for bog/mire flora, indicate the onset of a wetter climate. However, the human agencies linked with upland soil erosion due to intensive agricultural activity should not be ignored—the effects of deforestation and cultivation. Similar patterns within the pollen sequence occur throughout the peat and mire sites of central Wales. The environmental sequence by itself cannot be used to infer the involvement of human agency. There are, however, a few sites where the pollen evidence and archaeo-logical record can be correlated to reveal the interaction of environmental forces and anthropogenic activity. At Four Crosses, a pollen sequence from a buried soil dating to *c.*3310 + 70 BP (reference no: CAR-667) has indicated woodland clearance followed by intensive animal grazing and possible cereal cultivation prior to the construction of a barrow (Wimble 1986). A further pollen sequence has been identified in peat below the floor slab of a cist at Corn Du, dated 3695 + 75 BP (CAR-202). The evidence showed the cist was constructed in an open boggy landscape surrounded by localised scrub vegetation, indicating anthropogenic activity. Just south of the Black Mountains, soils from Bronze Age cairns at Crug-yr-Avan (Crampton 1967), Penrhyncoch (Smith & Taylor 1969) and Croesmihangel have indicated deforestation and, more important, soil deterioration.

More substantial remains, such as charcoal, wood, faunal remains and molluscs, are not so common. Notable finds include a Late Bronze Age dugout canoe, made from oak, discovered on Llyn Llangors. The presence of charcoal at a few locations may indicate the use of fire, perhaps to clear undergrowth, although natural causes, such as lightning strikes, may be responsible. Few animal remains can survive the acidic soils of this area. However, on the basis of evidence from other sites, such as Caldicot (South Wales) and Tooth Cave (Gower), ox, pig, sheep, horse and dog would have been present, together with red deer, brown hare, water vole and some water fowl such as mallard.

Dol y Felin

Standing Stone
Location: In the village of Llanafan-Fawr, appx. 5km south-west
of Newbridge on Wye (SN 977 550)
Access: On private land, but visible from the road

From the village of Newbridge on Wye (in Radnorshire) proceed southwards along the B4358 towards Beulah. Approximately 4km along this road at the hamlet of Llanafan-Fawr take a left turn past the church. About 1.2km along this road and visible from the road on the left is the Dol y Felin standing stone. Permission is required from the nearby farm before visiting this site.

The Dol y Felin standing stone (also referred to as St Arfan's Stone), standing at 185m OD traditionally marks the location where St Arfan (or St Arvan), a Welsh saint or bishop was supposedly murdered in the 6th century. According to a source within the RCAHM(W) there is an incised cross within a circle on one of its faces, but the authors could find no trace of this, due to the stone being heavily covered with lichen. The monument, basically rectangular in shape stands 2.18m in height and 1.53m in width (across its western face). The monument leans slightly to the north, possibly the result of subsidence, and rises to form a blunt point.

With regards to the landscape position, the Dol y Felin monument stands close to the Afon Chwefru and within marginal farmland. Approximately 2km to the north the landscape changes to upland moorland. A series of standing stones including Dol y Felin appear to flank the boundary between marginal pasture and moorland (other monuments include the destroyed Y Garth monolith (SN 949 558), the Llanfihangel Brynpabuan stone (SN 990 570) and the Llanwrthwl Church stone (SN 976 637). The line of standing stones, oriented roughly south-west/north-east encompasses an intense Bronze Age landscape which contains at least 20 cairns—all located on the highest points within the landscape.

Mynydd Bach Trecastell Stone Circles

Two stone circles
Location: In the hills some 4km north-west of Trecastell
(SN 833 311)
Access: By a decent walk over the hills

Heading west from Trecastell, take a second right through the village, where the old school is on the junction, proceeding up the hill for about 0.75km. Take the first right turn and continue for approximately 3.5km along what was once a Roman road (Coed y Dorallt). Approximately 2.5km along this road is a gated track and you want to park near here. Walk along the track for 1.5km. This track incorporates some of the most impressive landscapes in this part of Wales. The original road is still visible in places, especially the central section of the camber. Notice also the remarkable fossilised turfed embankments on either side. The road terminates at a trig. point 383m OD with a tumulus 10m to the north. Leave the road and proceed along a track for approximately 2km before following a track 0.5km to the north. At a point where two tracks converge, one veering to the west, walk along the northern track until fencing comes into view marking the boundary between moorland and upland pastures. Proceed north-west and both stone circles will become clearly visible, located on a small raised platform, or what the RCAHM(W) (1997) refers to as a 'curvilinear enclosure', comprising a small bank and ditch. Just north of this platform the land slopes gently to the north-east. Visiting the site one is privileged to find not only a prehistoric monument complex, but, a few metres farther west, the Roman camps of Y Pigwn and a Roman fortlet and motte at Waun Ddu. On the south-eastern slopes of the Y Pigwn Camp, and directly in view of the stone circles, is a series of linear banks and ditches which may be interpreted either as defence or boundary lines associated with the camp or as later field systems. Surrounding the whole area are many depressions which may be the result of quarrying or possible pockmarks from military training after the Second World War.

Although not properly surveyed until the 20th century, the monuments were discovered by John Rhys Jones in 1849 and reported in *Archaeologia Cambrensis* in 1854 (No. 8:125-34). Standing 44.2m apart at an elevation of 370m OD, the monuments appear to form a blueprint for other stone-circle pairs in this part of Wales. Ideas popularised by Alexander Thom (1967) suggest these

The Roman road

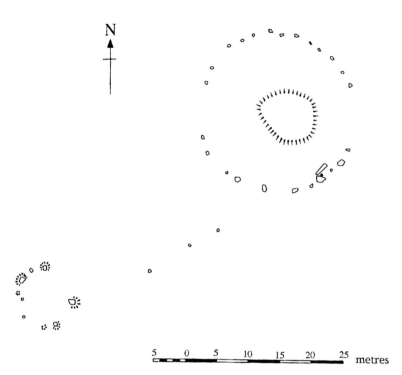

N

| 5 | 0 | 5 | 10 | 15 | 20 | 25 | metres |

Plan of the stone circles and stones 'linking' them

and similar structures had astronomical functions. Between the circles, which are of Old Red Sandstone, is a line of three stones ranging in height from 0.4m to 0.64m. These may have some ritual significance either linking the circles or, in our opinion, defining a processional route between the monuments. The eastern circle, comprising 21 regularly-spaced stones 0.1m-0.5m high, is 23.2m in diameter and slightly elliptical. A number of pits suggest the complete circle once possessed at least 25 stones. There appears to be a possible ritual entrance within the south-east section (Burnham 1995), whilst in the centre is evidence of a possible burial mound measuring 6.8m in diameter (north-west/south-east). The smaller circle is approximately 8m in diameter. This consists of four uprights, all of which have splayed outwards, standing about 0.9m high—over time, their settings have become eroded and, on the southern section, water has collected to reveal packing stones. In addition, we have identified a further three stones and there are five sockets indicating missing stones. The two circles are aligned north-west/south-east and point towards a small hillock to the north-east, taking in extensive views of the Cwm Dwr. Farther west and south-west are two cairns, which are probably contemporary with the circles. To the south, further cairns and two standing stones hint at the existence of a complete Bronze Age ritual landscape, although (and we regard this as an important point) there is no inter-visibility, no visual link, between the circles and other monuments, except perhaps for the two nearby cairns. It could well be that more monumental stones within the immediate landscape await discovery. The authors have noted two possible recumbent standing stones north-west of the Roman road, at the point where the field boundaries leave the track.

Troed Rhiw Wen

Standing Stone
Location: On the edge of the moorland south-west
of Trecastell (SN 836 256)
Access: Visible from the road, but can be reached
across the moor

From Trecastell, head south-west towards the small settlement of Beiliaugleision, indicated by a 'T' no-through road sign. From this settlement continue south-west along a winding track towards the Glasfynydd Forest. To the south, the forest stops and moorland begins. Approximately 200m from this point, on a gradual slope in an area known as Garn Las, is the Troed Rhiw Wen stone, which is clearly visible from the road.

This large, squared monolith of Old Red Sandstone stands approximately 343m OD 1.67m above the existing ground level on a small plateau. Around the stone is a series of small boulders which may derive from the top and sides of the stone, alternatively, they may be part of the extensive field clearance within this area.

The stone, rectangular in plan (measuring 1.35m east/west by 0.93m wide) has a flat top. A similarly shaped stone (measuring 0.8m x 0.41m x 1.7m long) lies recumbent a few metres west on the same terrace. Approximately 1.8km to the west of the monolith are two stone circles and a single cairn. To the south-south-west is a further series of stone circles and cairns along the summit of Fan Brycheiniog. These monuments clearly form part of an extensive Bronze Age landscape. Between the standing stone and the stone circles to the west is a small stream, Nant Traw, which appears to divide the monuments within the landscape. It is likely that further monuments stood within the area that is now part of the Glasfynydd Forest. This area was probably heavily wooded during the Early Neolithic, but was cleared during the Bronze Age for cultivation.

Cerrig Duon Stone Circle

Stone Circle
Location: 10km south of Trecastell (SN 851 206)
Access: It lies some 30m from a road, and is reached across the
Afon Tawe via stepping stones, on which caution is required

From Trecastell, take a left turning opposite the post office towards
Abercraf. Proceed along this road for approximately 10km. The
road runs parallel to a series of rapids on the right-hand side.
Immediately above, one can glimpse the Maen Mawr ('Big Stone')
standing stone. This monument lies a few metres north of the stone
circle. Visitors should exercise caution when crossing the Afon
Tawe.

This monument, together with a stone row and the substantial
Maen Mawr, lies on a small plateau 380m OD within the Afon
Tawe Valley. The dramatic ridge of Fan Hir rises to the west. The
RCAHM(W) report (1997) suggests a series of non-ritual monuments lies close by, including field banks and hut circles. Stone
circle, standing stone and stone row are arranged in a north-south
linear configuration, aligned with the Afon Tawe. Stone rows are
common in other parts of Britain, including Exmoor and Dartmoor

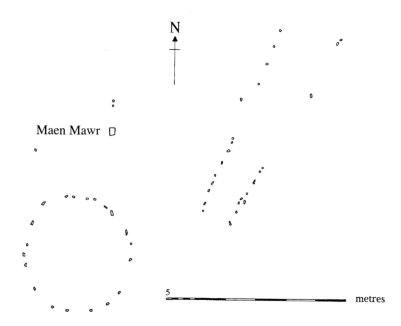

The Cerrig Duon Stone Circle and the Maen Mawr standing stone and stone row (adapted from the RCAHM[W])

and the present example consists of two converging alignments running roughly north-north-east/south-south-west from a point approximately 23m east-north-east of the centre of the circle. Both western and eastern rows are approximately 45m long and each consists of at least 16 stones (CPAT SMR). The feature narrows as it approaches the standing stone and stone circle as if defining a processional route leading up to the stone circle. It is probable that the stone circle, standing stone and two outliers, plus the stone row, are contemporary and created a special place of ritual and ceremony, incorporating a number of significant landscape features, including the Afon Tawe, which flows a few metres to the north-east of the stone row. About 1km north-north-east is a single standing stone known as Waen Lleuci (SN 855 215), 450m OD, which may also be considered part of the complex (see separate entry on p.112). On either side of the stone circle complex is a series of, probably contemporary, outlying cairns. A series of trackways, again running north-south past the complex, has been recognised (Grimes 1951). However, these are probably medieval roads used by drovers and pack-horses (RCAHM[W] 1997).

The circle complex, elliptical in form (Alexander Thom's Type 1 - egg shape) is made up of 20 visible stones of which one is recumbent. Between 1907 and 1936 there were 21 stones, one having since been removed on the south side of the monument. More stones are visible when conditions are dry and plant life depleted (Burnham 1995). The tallest stones rise no more than 0.6m above present ground height. The stones are evenly arranged in a slightly elliptical pattern, diameter 18.5m (north-south) x 17.5m (east-west), with an average spacing of 1.3m (RCAHM[W] 1997). The stones' slab-like appearance is accounted for by their being of Pennant Sandstone.

Approximately 10m north of the circle is the Maen Mawr stone, which stands, with evidence of packing stones, in a small, weather-eroded depression. More than 1.9m high, it must once have had a direct relationship with the circle. Indeed, when viewing both monuments from the north, the standing stone cuts directly through the centre of the circle and is aligned with a central point within the landscape where the lower part of the Tawe valley converges from the east and west. To reinforce this observation, a further two small outlying stones, again oriented north/south line up with the standing stone, the bisected stone circle and the lower part of the valley.

Positioned north-north-east of both monuments, some 14m from the standing stone, is a double stone row or avenue, 5m apart at the southern end, which funnels out from both monuments towards the northern section of the valley (possibly incorporating the Waen Lleuci standing stone). Some of the stones to the north on the eastern row have fallen away or remain buried. This monument is probably also contemporary with the standing stone and circle and, as argued earlier, may have formed part of a ritual procession route, either to or from the stone circle. However, as the stone row appears slightly tangential to the circle, it is possible that the two may be unrelated (Burnham 1995).

Maen Llia Standing Stone

© BBNP

Standing Stone
Location: On high moorland in the Fforest Fawr mountains,
south of Sennybridge (SN 924 192)
Access: Visible from the road and reached across a stile

If there was any monument that was in the middle of nowhere, this
is it! From Brecon, proceed along the A470 towards Cefn-coed-y-
cymmer and Merthyr Tydfil. Approximately 6km along this road
proceed west onto the A4215 towards Sennybridge. Head along this
road for 3.75km and take a left turn signposted 'Heol Senni'. Drive

through the village and across the Afon Senni and take the first left turn (south) to Neuadd. About 5km along this road and crossing the Afon Senni from west to east and venturing onto upland heath, the Maen Llia standing stone (and related cairns) is clearly visible, approximately 50m from the road on the left.

This monument, trapezoidal-shaped, stands over 3.60m in height and 2.76m broad. It is sited within a shallow depression, possibly the result of sheep sheltering from the frequent adverse weather conditions. The stone is made from a conglomerate sandstone and stands over 430m OD, close to the source of the Afon Llia. According to Macalister (1922) faint inscriptions on the lower right of the monument's western face show possible Roman characters, reading ROVEVI / S....SOVI; and VASSO (G?) (it should be noted that a Roman road runs some 300m east of this monument).

Legend suggests that Maen Llia loves fresh water and goes for a drink in the Afon Nedd when it hears the crowing of the cock (Barber & Williams 1989:176). It should be cynically noted that there are very few cocks within this area of Breconshire.

The monument stands within a marshy upland plateau between two mountains—Fan Llia and Fan Nedd. Surrounding the stone are a number of cairns, all intervisible (at SN 918 189; SN 918 179; SN 927 189 and SN 936 183). Maen Llia and the cairns are probably contemporary—most likely dating to the Middle to Late Bronze Age (c.1600 - 1000 BC). It is probable that the monumentality of such a monument as Maen Llia coincided with ritual activity involving the cairns, in particular burial practice and the movement of the deceased from a known point within the landscape (the standing stone) to a final resting place—the cairn.

Saith Maen Stone Row

© BBNP

Stone row
Location: Close to the Dan-yr-Ogof show caves (SN 833 154)
Access: Permission to visit is needed from nearby
Nant gwared Farm

The Saith Maen stone row is located 700m west-south-west of Nant gwared Farm, close to a dismantled tramway and 20m south of a track that leads from the A4067 south of the farm.

This enigmatic monument sits within a unique limestone landscape of rock outcropping and shake holes that form a typical karst landscape. The area also includes the remains of a little known industrial development of early post-medieval settlements and 19th-century limestone quarries, mine shafts and tramways which litter this bare and exposed landscape.

The Saith Maen (in English: Severn Stones) stone row is comprised of seven equidistant stones, two of which are now recumbent (4th and 6th setting). The complete alignment extends some 12m. The stones (including those recumbent) range from 0.6m to 2.8m in height and are set in shallow depressions, possibly the result of sheep activity. Each stone, with the exception of the 3rd setting is cut from Carboniferous siliceous grit stone. The 3rd setting, a rounded boulder, is formed from Old Red Sandstone and was either dragged to its present position from an Old Red Sandstone outcrop or may have been simply a glacial erratic.

It is probable that the present stones, oriented north-north-east by south-south-west form only part of what was a complex stone alignment. This alignment may have linked other monuments such as a nearby cairn (SN 829 151) and hut circle (SN 828 152) to the south with further cairns (SN 835 168 and SN 837 172) and a possible Late Bronze Age field system and hut circles (SN 837 177). Many of these monuments are intervisible with Saith Maen. Barber & Williams (1989:181) suggest that the alignment extends to the stone circle of Cerrig Duon, some 6km to the north-east.

The site has dramatic views across the landscape (especially to the south) and is typically sited on one of the highest points in the immediate landscape. It also stands within an area of upland which is covered with a thin layer of peat, an important palaeoenvironmental resource presently under threat from tourism and intensive grazing. The peat is the result of probable Middle to Late Bronze Age land clearance followed by cultivation and then prehistoric climatic deterioration. The peats overlie leached whitish grey silica dominant glacial clays and gravels.

Theophilus Jones in 1809 remarked that the stones formed part of a sheepfold.

Waen Lleuci

Standing Stone
Location: 8km south of Trecastell (SN 854 215)
Access: Can be seen from the road

From Trecastell, proceed south towards Abercraf. Approximately 8km along this mountain road, and just before a stone circle complex, is Waen Lleuci, located on the eastern side about 300m from the road from which it is visible. This single monolith stands approximately 1.95m tall and is 1.52m in width by 0.26m in thickness. It has been squared at the top and is heavily covered with lichen.

This monument is associated with the stone circle 1km to the north and the Maen Mawr monolith to the south and is also possibly associated with a series of cairns to the north and west near the slopes of Fan Brycheiniog, probably marking a processional route between these monuments. Undoubtedly, this standing stone is contemporary with other monuments standing in this valley and the surrounding moorland. Made of Old Red Sandstone, it is intervisible with the Cerrig Duon stone circle and monolith and stands on a small plateau about 15m in diameter on the slopes of Waen Lleuci, 450m OD.

Nant Tarw Stone Circles

Two stone circles
Location: By the Usk Reservoir, south of Trecastell
(SN 818 258)
Access: On open moorland, so be prepared

Stout boots and good weather are needed to visit this site. Take the turning off the A40 opposite Trecastell Post Office towards the Usk Reservoir and proceed along the country lane for about 10km, passing the reservoir to the north. Park when you reach the parking point at a cattle grid on the edge of some woodland. The stone circles can be found 3km due south-west of Foel Darw, a large hill (424m OD).

From the car park, proceed south along the edge of the Mynydd Wysg forestry area. Five hundred metres further on, turn due east towards the upper section of the river Usk. Proceed along the stream until reaching an interfluve of the Usk and the Nant Tarw. Walk between the two streams for approximately 0.75km. Directly south is a small plateau and the dramatic scarps of Picws Du and Fan Brycheiniog. The two circles are located 350m OD on a small platform overlooking the Nant Tarw. The western circle (Circle A) is the higher of the two. Both are aligned north-west/south-east. To the north of the eastern circle (Circle B) are the remains of a large, robbed cairn, a stone setting, monolith and embanked enclosure. A number of settlement features, in the form of raised platforms, suggest the presence of a farming community during medieval times, when the climate was slightly warmer and population densities were higher than at present. Charcoal flecks beneath a plough-soil profile from just north of the complex may indicate prehistoric or medieval clearance.

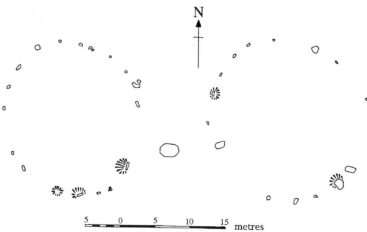

Nant Tarw stone circles, Circle A on the left and B on the right

Set just over 110m apart, the circles were investigated in the 1960s (Dorling 1996). The slightly elliptical Circle A is 19.3m in diameter and comprises 15 stones, the highest standing 0.7m high, and a possible post-hole on the southern section. The stones and associated sockets are evenly spaced, with breaks at the east and west, which Grimes suggests may be deliberate, hinting at the presence of an entrance/exit. Circle A comprises glacial boulders and underlying Old Red Sandstone slabs. Four boulders are completely buried (RCAHM[W] 1997:150). Approximately 3m west of Circle A, roughly central to the open section of the circle and south of the axial line between the circle centres, lies a fallen stone 2.6m long. Circle B, which is again slightly elliptical, measures 21m x 18.5m in diameter and has 18 visible stones, the highest rising 0.8m. This circle too has an incomplete circumference, with two seven-metre

gaps in the south-east and south-west sections. To the west, lies another possible recumbent standing stone or natural glacial erratic overlying moraine debris (Burnham 1995:44).

Although occupying a low-lying platform, the circles offer dramatic views of the surrounding glacial landscape, particularly to the south. Large patches of marshy ground may have formed a natural boundary controlling the immediate space around both monuments. A further 4km south of the Nant Tawr stone circles, at the foot of Fan Brycheiniog (802m OD), stands another similar

monument, while two cairns stand atop the escarpment, from which vantage point the circles and their associated features are clearly visible.

About 90m directly north of Circle B and standing at an elevation of some 410m OD is a robbed cairn, consisting of a substantial stone scatter approximately 0.3m high. The cairn measures 16m x 11m. Large fallen slabs may be the remains of a cist (RCAHM[W] 1997:78).This monument has suffered badly over the last 90 years or so, for antiquarian accounts indicate that five or six erect stones once defined its circumference. Directly north of the cairn, and on the southern side of the Nant Tarw, is a possible standing stone measuring 1.6m high. Again, this unobtrusive monument may once have possessed an important ritual significance in relation to the stone circle and cairn to the south, acting as a processional marker.

Llwyn y Fedwen Standing Stone

Standing Stone
Location: Near Talybont on Usk (SO 156 204)
Access: On private land

From Talybont (on the B4558) turn west towards a monastic building known as Gileston. Beyond this, the monolith stands approximately 200m to the north on an ancient river terrace.

This large monolith, one of a number of stones within the area, stands 4.27m high and is one of the tallest in this part of Wales. Referred to as Llwyn y Fedwen, it is sited between the river Usk and the Monmouthsire and Brecon Canal. Located on a small, natural knoll measuring 65m long by 4m high and 107m OD, this monolith is within a hedge boundary and is made of erratic limestone. It is reported that a large number of stones were placed against the monolith in the 1930s and were still there in 1985— possibly part of successive field clearances. The RCAHM(W) report (1997) notes that this monolith, which leans to the north, was used as a possible marker for the Brecon monks' tithe lands during the 13th century.

Carreg Waun Llech Standing Stone

© BBNP

Standing Stone
Location: On the hills south of Llangynidr (SO 164 174)
Access: On private land, but visible from the road

From Llangynidr take the B4558 east towards Llangattock. Approximately 0.75km along this road, turn south onto the B4560, signposted Beaufort. Proceed along this road for 3.5km and take the first left turn, heading north-east for about 1km. Carreg Waun Llech standing stone is located 200m from this road on the left on a south-east facing slope.

The site was first noted on a map produced by E. Bowen in 1729 and referred to as 'Croes Sion Kusmon' (translated as 'a collection of stones'). Carreg Waun Llech is formed from a large weathered (conglomerate) limestone block sited within marshland on a large limestone plateau and is located at 387m OD. The stone stands 2.64m in height and is 1.28m broad by 0.45m in depth. On its eastern face it has a series of weathered vertical jointing lines as well as a number of pitted holes which resemble small cupmarks, but these holes form part of the weathering process. Around the base of the stone is evidence of stone packing and/or cairn clearance activity. It has been suggested by the RCAHM(W) that this stone also formed a probable medieval boundary marker between the parishes of Llangatwg and Llangynidr (1997:174).

This standing stone is located within extensive open upland heath and probably forms part of an extensive Bronze Age ritual landscape. Close by to the south and east are a number cairns located along the Craig y Cilau ridge (SO 19 15), Mynydd Llangatwg (SO 19 14) and Mynydd Llangynidr (SO 12 15). It also stands between the fertile valleys of the River Usk to the north and the extensive uplands of Mynydd Llangynidr and Mynydd Llangatwg to the south. The areas in which both sets of cairns are located can be seen from the standing stone. Further standing stones, such as the Fish Stone (SO 183 199) and the standing stone at Bwlch are located some 5km to the north.

Fish Stone

Standing Stone
Location: Near Penmyarth Church, north-west of Crickhowell
(SO 183 199)
Access: On private land by the river Usk

The Fish Stone, standing next to the River Usk and close to Penmyarth Church is one of a number of impressive standing stones within the Usk Valley between Bwlch and Crickhowell. From Crickhowell head north-west along the A40 towards Bwlch. Approximately 2.75km along this road, and shortly after the junction with the A479, turn south along a country lane signposted 'Llangynidr'. About 400m along this road, follow a footpath to Penmyarth Church. From the church, proceed westwards along the line of the river Usk. The Fish Stone is located some 350m west of the church and within Penmyarth Park. It lies alongside a private path along the rover bank.

The Fish Stone, so-named because of its fish-shaped form is located near the northern bank of the River Usk, with its tail touching the ground. Legend suggests that the stone jumps into the river on Midsummer Eve in order to go for a swim (Barber & Williams 1989:67). The monument stands 4.27m high, 1.24m broad and 0.40m in depth, and is regarded as one of Wales' tallest standing stones (or menhirs). Cut from Old Red Sandstone, it is believed that it was quarried from outcrops located south of the River Usk (*ibid.* 166). The standing stone stands on top of a steep rise, approximately 8m from the Usk and appears to be embedded into both the sub-soils and, possibly, the bedrock. This being the case, the total length of this monument must be close on 6m.

The stone is first mentioned by Theophilus Jones in his *A History of Brecknock* of 1805-09 and later on in a lease between William Augustus Gott to Thomas Johnson in 1825. The RCAHM(W) make reference that this stone is a Medieval parish boundary marker (1997:174).

The Fish Stone forms part of an extensive group of monuments that flank the northern side of the River Usk. The valley position of this stone and other nearby tall standing stones, especially Cwt-y-gollen (SO 213 169) and the standing stone at Llanfihangel Cwm Du (SO 156 204) appear to suggest primary markers which lead to other standing stones to the north, which in turn lead towards cairns at, for example, Mynydd Llangors (SO 160 251), Pen Gloch-y-pibwr (SO 203 233) and Pen Cerrig-calch (SO 217 223).

Cwrt y Gollen monolith

Standing Stone
Location: Between Crickhowell and Abergavenny (SO 212 168)
Access: Visible from the A40

Located 65m OD within the entrance area of Cwrt y Gollen Army Training School this large, single, Old Red Sandstone monolith stands about 4.17m high. The monument is fenced and set within an ornamental cobbled pavement. The authors suggest this was not the original position, although it does appear to be part of a standing stone tradition which follows along the northern banks of the Usk between Brecon and Crickhowell.

Llanfihangel Cwm Du monolith

> Standing Stone
> Location: North of Tretower (SO 180 219)
> Access: Can be seen from the road

From Crickhowell proceed north along the A40. Take a right turning along the A479 signposted Talgarth. Approximately 1.5km past the village of Tretower, and on the left hand side, is the monolith.

This monument, one of a number within this part of the Usk Valley, commands dominating views to the south and east. There appears to be no direct intervisibility with other standing stones but it does conform to our theory that it 'acts' as a marker for movement of people through the landscape. Standing 135m OD, this impressive monument, now within a field boundary, stands 2.25m high, and like other monoliths within the area is rectangular in section, measuring 1.15m in width (north/south) and 0.86m east/west. Made from a conglomerate sandstone, it leans slightly to the west. Close by to the south-west is another monolith also known by the same name which stands approximately 2.34m high.

Blaenau Stone Circle

> Stone Circle
> Location: At the foot of Hay Bluff (SO 239 373)
> Access: Car park situated right along side!

From Hay-on-Wye, take the B4350 and head west, turning left in the town where it is signposted 'Capel y ffin' and continue along the minor road, making one right turn, for approximately 6.5km. After passing a small cairn on the left, the Blaenau Stone Circle can be found close to a car park on the right, close to the foot of Hay Bluff (Blaen Diyedi). Located on a large area of common land forming part of a plateau, the circle and its surroundings have been subject to recent quarrying, possibly the result of metal detecting. The site has also been damaged by the encroachment of the car park and the eastern section has now been protected by a row of boulders. Very few stones are visible, but the site does offer outstanding views across the upper Wye Valley to the west and Hay Bluff, a dramatic escarpment of the Black Mountains, to the east. The monument's position, and the presence of associated cairns and standing stones nearby, suggests a similarity with other Bronze Age complexes further west.

An ancient monument has long been suspected on this site, but it was not until 1970 that its existence was conclusively revealed. The site was originally thought to be the remains of a burial chamber owing to the presence of a large upright slab and the stubs of a few adjacent stones (Dorling 1996:6). The circle comprises 18 visible stones, standing at varying heights above the turf, and is located on a flat plateau below Pen y Beacon. Overlooking the Digedi Brook Valley, the circle is one of the largest in the county, measuring 29.8m in diameter. Two of the largest stones are set radially and define what appears to be a small entrance/exit within the eastern section, pointing directly towards the summit of Hay Bluff. This is a rare feature among Welsh stone circles. Furthermore, on the base of one of the stones is a single cupmark measuring 7cm diameter and 3cm deep, which may be the handiwork of the original builders (Dorling 1996) or later 'graffiti'. Just above the cupmark is an OS benchmark indicating a height of 470m above

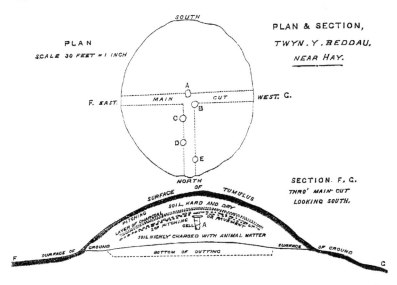

Twyn y beddau measures roughly 8m in diameter and is found next to the mountain road between Hay-on-Wye and the stone circle, was excavated in the 19th century. The plan and section drawn by antiquarians is one of a handful of drawings made on ths type of monument

sea level. A hut circle of ruinous drystone walling has been identified close by. The wall itself is around 1.3m wide, with an entrance on the south side. This structure is adjacent to a rectangular hut feature (Primary Record Number 35831) within the northern part of the enclosure.

Probably associated with the stone circle are a number of monuments that roughly date from the same period and reinforce the idea of a procession between monuments. Approximately 500m north from the Blaenau stone circle is Twyn y beddau, a large Bronze Age cairn. To the east of this cairn and the stone circle, and located along the plateau below Hay Bluff, are a number of stones which may be merely glacial erratics.

The Iron Age

The Legacy of Plundering the Land:
Environmental considerations

The Iron Age is regarded as a time of climatic deterioration, with higher rainfall (Taylor 1980b). There was a marked increase in peat formation in the form of raised bogs in upland areas, a process that may have begun as early as the mid- to late Bronze Age. Over-intensive agricultural use of the upland slopes coupled with higher rainfall degraded existing field systems, at the same time increasing the alluvial content of the river valleys. Consideration of these environmental factors is crucial to understanding how Iron Age society functioned. Unfortunately, there has been little discussion of the palaeoenvironmental evidence relating to the Iron Age in Breconshire, which makes any overall assessment difficult. However, surrounding sites offer some useful indicators (Caseldine 1990:71-3). The most illuminating is Caer Cadwgan, near Lampeter, Cardiganshire, which has yielded pollen, carbonised plant remains and animal bone. The intensification of landscape use is apparent in the extensive clearances of hazel and scrub, which may have been due to the need for virgin land. At the upland site of Waun-figcn-felen, there is evidence of woodland regeneration during the early Iron Age followed by clearance around 200 BC (Smith & Cloutman 1988). The presence of plantain pollen (*plantago lanceolata*) indicates a burst of arable activity not dissimilar from that apparent during the Neolithic. In the Black Mountains, at Pen y Gader Fawr and Ty Isaf, plantain remains are dated to between 500 BC and 100 BC respectively (Moore *et al*. 1984). The climatic downturn brought other localised environmental changes, with oak, hazel and birch initially colonising the valley sides and floors; and whilst alder survived on the wetter valley floor much arboreal pollen is replaced by herbaceous pollen, including that of cereal. A change in the pollen record can be seen at Llangorse Lake, where arable activity led to increased soil erosion around the Llynfi catchment during the later Iron Age and the early period of Roman occupation (Jones *et al.* 1985).

Setting the Scene - 800 BC to 55 BC and beyond
Iron appears in significant quantities in the artefactual record towards the end of the Bronze Age, but bronze remained the more fashionable metal and continued to be used for items of personal adornment, such as pins and, later, brooches used as clothes fastenings. The latter became widespread from the 5th century BC, with early Continental types diversifying into a range of insular forms. A profusion of rings, bracelets and beads further testifies to the importance of personal appearance. The artistic temperament of the Celtic peoples, increasingly apparent from about 500 BC onwards, also found expression in weaponry. Following a period during which daggers became fashionable, swords with highly decorated scabbards gradually evolved local and regional variants. These weapons were regarded as more than instruments of death or status symbols, as suggested by finds of swords and other metalwork that had been (ritually) deposited in water, a tradition echoed in the legend of Excalibur. Attention was also lavished on eating and drinking. Abundant Iron Age pottery includes a range of more elaborate feasting vessels, while cauldron-hangers and firedogs indicate the importance of hearth and home. Other materials were used to fashion everyday items and structures, including clay (pottery, loom weights, spindle-whorls and sling-shots), stone (quernstones and whetstones), bone (weaving combs and needles) and wood (ploughshares, houses, fences and trackways).

The Iron Age, unlike the Neolithic and Bronze Ages, was also a period when the economy and settlement were more visible than death, which virtually disappears from the archaeological record around this time. This shift of emphasis from the dead to the living appears to be accompanied by a movement of people from the intermediate slopes and uplands to the river valleys and foothill margins. Hillforts, or what we prefer to term 'hill enclosures', remain the most visible legacy of the Celtic, or Celticised, peoples of Wales and the Marches, but quite where these stood in the local settlement hierarchy remains very much open to question. Folklore and antiquarian studies are rife with attempts to explain the origin of these massive earthworks. A proliferation of 'Caesar's Camps' can be traced back to the 17th century (Hogg, 1975), while earlier traditions link enclosures with the name of Arthur (e.g. South Cadbury) or the British resistance hero Caratacus (enclosures bearing the name 'Caer Caradoc' — 'stronghold of Caratacus' — can be found near Clun, at Church Stretton and at Llanfihangel-Glyn-Myfry). With the growth of scientific archaeology in the 20th century, efforts were made to bring an objective focus to the question of origins. In particular, radiocarbon dating has been used to underpin a much more rigorous chronology. Systematic dating of gateway sequences, for example, has revealed a series of early enclosures in the central Marches. Much pioneering work was carried out at Croft Ambrey, Herefordshire, where the first 'defences' were established around 550 BC (Stanford 1991). At The Breiddin, Montgomeryshire, where finds include Bronze Age pins and a socketed axe and hammer, even earlier traces of occupation have been dated to 868 +/- 64 bc and 754 +/- 50 bc. As Stanford says: 'Whereas these camps were once viewed as a late reaction to the Roman invasion, the chronological bracket has expanded dramatically' (1991:43). Although conventionally viewed as defended settlements, our research in Herefordshire and Monmouthshire (Children & Nash 1994 & 1996) has led us to interpret hill enclosures principally as monuments signifying status and the ownership of land. They thus had an important symbolic role in the emergence and consolidation of territories. As for specific functions, these may have included use as cattle corrals, trade and exchange centres or sites for the processing of agricultural products. That is, these enclosures were places where particular activities were carried out, rather than sites of permanent habitation. Alcock (1965), for example, has suggested hill enclosures in this part of the world may have served as stations for cattle and sheep herders as they moved between upland summer pastures and the more sheltered lowlands. The size of each enclosure may relate to the potential productivity of the tribal area concerned, although there is no clear correlation. It is likely that Iron Age people in this area practised a mixed farming economy, with local topography influencing the relative importance of arable and pastoral. Although a shift from large enclosures to smaller dispersed farmsteads has been suggested (Mytum 1988), we would argue that both were in use at the same time, but that they had different roles. Smaller enclosures, interpreted as farmsteads, may have have been used more for grain processing and storage. It should be noted, too, that two large hill enclosures in Herefordshire—Croft Ambrey and Midsummer Hill—revealed evidence of four-post structures, which may be grain drying houses (Stanford 1991). We should not be confused by previous research concerning population dynamics in relation to 'hill fort' occupation as expressed by Stanford, who promotes the idea that hillfort size and distance from others provides the basis for calculating population density.

Tribal Distribution

In terms of language, material culture and possibly religious beliefs the Celts formed a single European culture, although this apparent homogeneity probably concealed a good deal of diversity, with more ancient traditions dominating towards the Atlantic fringe. As D.W. Harding has observed, '... there can be little doubt that the British Iron Age from its inception retained a strong native component'. (Harding 1974:134). Savory envisages 'an extraneous, strongly Celtic culture' with 'large well-organised and fortified villages' developing in the central and northern Marches while 'a largely indigenous culture' continued to occupy scattered farmsteads in central and southern Wales (1980(b):288/9). These areas translate into the different tribal domains later identified by the Romans.

An earlier invasion/migration scenario was proposed by A.H. Williams (1941), who wrote that 'the practice of hillfort building is now thought to have been introduced to Wales during the last few centuries of the prehistoric era by Celtic immigrants who came here from Devon and Somerset via the Bristol Channel and Severn Valley'. Similarly, the arrival of iron-working is explained in terms of migrants imposing a new technology on native peoples. Given developments in chronology, Williams' scenario is clearly defective; some hill enclosures may have their origins in the Bronze Age, while the transition to iron may simply have been the outcome of a need to keep pace with the growing demand for metalwork. In the decades since A.H. Williams' book appeared, there has been much resistance to the migration scenario. Since the 1960s, at least in Britain and America, the emphasis has shifted away from migration as an explanation of social change towards the role of internal factors, although there is evidence that the pendulum is beginning to swing back. The migrationist model fell out of favour following the decline of western colonialism. By the same token, renewed interest in recent years may have been influenced by contemporary refugee movements (Chapman 1997). The neo-migrationists differ from their forebears in recognising migration as a complex phenomenon. What might be termed the traditional scenario of 'hordes of warriors, armed with better (and cheaper) weapons of iron, setting up fortified invasion bases' is, as Hogg (1975:47) implies, undoubtedly simplistic. Instead, one might imagine a complex series of cross-Channel relationships (social, economic, political, military) facilitating the sharing of ideas between Britain and Western Europe. The Iron Age societies of mid-Wales could thus have assimilated external influences without necessarily having change forced upon them. As Stanford observes, '... prehistoric communities often acquired objects and ideas from afar and communications seem to have been comparatively efficient' (1991:43). This approach appears to form the basis of ideas 'invading' an area and replacing the classic 'diffusionist' models expressed during the middle part of the 20th. century.

Iron Age Britain seems to have comprised a number of tribal territories. Where present-day Breconshire fitted into the political scene is uncertain. To the north-west, it is said, lay the lands of the Ordovices, while the Cornovii occupied modern Shropshire and parts of Staffordshire, Cheshire, Clwyd and the eastern portion of Powys. A neighbouring tribe, the Dobunni, may have extended their influence as far west as Herefordshire, while the lands of the formidable Silures of South Wales (described by Tacitus as dark-skinned and curly-haired and quite different in appearance from other British populations) may have included southern Powys. Quite where the eastern boundary of Silurean territory lay is again open to speculation. It has recently been suggested (Manning) that the 'tribe' extended their influence as far east as Herefordshire. Alternatively, Savory suggests the Silures occupied a territory to the south of a belt of forest stretching from Herefordshire to south Radnorshire (1980a: 304).

The Silures stand out as being particularly forceful in defence of their independence. Their extreme hostility to Rome sparked a bitter and protracted struggle, culminating in AD52 with the defeat of a legion. Symbolising British resistance to Roman domination during the middle years of the first century AD is the figure of Caratacus (Caradoc), who led a ferocious campaign against the Roman governor Publius Ostorius Scapula, transferring the war from South Wales northwards to the lands of the Ordovices. The final battle is said to have taken place on the River Severn, near Newtown. Others believe the scene of Caratacus' final stand was the hill enclosure of Coxall Knoll, near Leintwardine, in Herefordshire. Further claimants include the three Caer Caradocs previously mentioned, near Clun, Church Stretton and Llanfihangel-Glyn-Myfry. Wherever the battle was fought, Caratacus and his followers suffered an over-whelming defeat. His family was captured, while Caratacus himself managed to escape, only to be betrayed to the enemy shortly after-wards by Cartimandua, a female Celtic ruler and collaborator. Despite Caratacus' capture, however, the Silures continued to oppose Rome and briefly managed to attract other tribes to form an anti-Roman confederacy. Following further campaigns against the Silures by Q. Veranius (AD57-8) and his successor Suetonius Paulinus, they were finally subdued and Romanised under the governorship of Sextus Julius Frontinus (AD74-8), when it is said they were moved from their native fortress at Llanmelin to a new Roman town three kilometres away at Caerwent. Breconshire's three known Roman forts—Caerau, Llangamarch; Y Gaer, Brecon; and Pen-y-Gaer—together with three or four marching camps, may date from this period.

Celtic social organisation:
Warriors, farmers and 'howling priests'
Warriors and druids comprised two of the main classes of Celtic society. Beneath them in status were those who produced and those who served. Celtic warriors were regarded by the writers of antiq-

uity as almost childlike in their arrogance and love of self-display. Their behaviour and attitude to death were influenced by the teachings of the druids, the Celtic priesthood, who have been surrounded by a romantic aura since earliest times. The druids taught of the continuity of life after death, a belief that is said to have inspired warriors to reckless bravery. They seem to have been most active in Britain and parts of France, where they were accorded high status. They are associated with secret forest groves, where certain trees — the oak, ash and yew — were venerated. In these isolated places, human sacrifices may have been offered to the gods. Rituals may also have been performed near rivers or other watery places, regarded with reverence since at least the Middle Bronze Age, where substantial votive deposits of metalwork have been found. A symbolic link between the human skull and water is preserved in Welsh legend. It is said, for example, that when St Lludd was decapitated a spring burst from the rock against which the severed head came to rest. Skulls have also been found in deep shafts, which, like wells, were probably regarded as entrances to the underworld, although associations with fertility are also possible. Becoming a druid was not an exclusively male privilege, for women could also enter the order. There were also female seers — those possessing the power of prophecy and divination. Indeed, the role of women generally in what appeared to be a male-dominated world was not altogether subordinate, and the rise of female warleaders such as Cartimandua proves women could attain positions of power and influence. Apart from their religious influence, the druids seem to have played a prominent political role. In some parts of Wales, they whipped up opposition to Rome, playing so heavily on the doctrine of the immortal soul that warriors became convinced of their immunity.

While warriors boasted of battles won and priests, hidden away in their mysterious sacred groves, engaged in arcane religious practices, the bulk of the population laboured to produce the surpluses needed to support them. The typical settlement unit, in Breconshire as elsewhere in southern Britain, was the farmstead, comprising one or several houses constructed of timber, thatch and daub with accompanying storage in the form of pits and granaries. The most famous Iron Age farmstead is Little Woodbury, Wiltshire, which

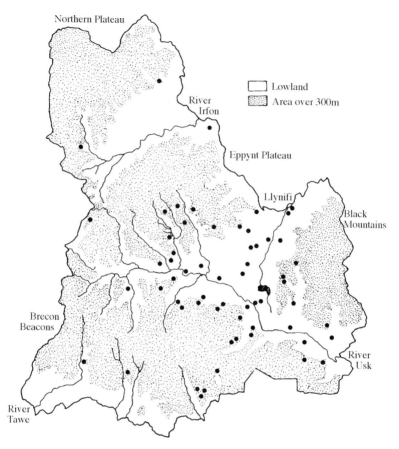

Distribution of Iron Age hill enclosures

comprised a central round house, granaries and pits enclosed by a palisade and ditch. Revised dating has pushed this settlement back to the 6th century BC and aerial survey has further revealed fairly dense activity within the vicinity. Within Breconshire, a number of small enclosures are known which may fall into the category of single farmsteads, some of which may have their origins in the Late Bronze Age (RCAHM[W] 1986).

After about the middle of the first millennium BC there were widespread forest clearances in England and Wales. The introduction of winter sown cereals heralded a greater control over food supply, an increase in population and more land being brought under the plough. Draught cattle were harnessed to ploughs which, lacking a mould board, merely scratched the surface of the soil rather than turning it over in furrows and fields had to be ploughed in two directions so as to break up the soil sufficiently for sowing. On hillsides, soil would tend to creep downhill, accumulating to form a bank or lynchet and such features can still be seen delineating field systems. After ploughing and sowing came the harvest. Ears of corn were cut from stalks with iron sickles, cleaned, threshed and stored. After the harvest, livestock was brought in from outlying pastures and river meadows to forage in the stubble fields. Cattle, sheep and pigs (whose rooting activity broke up the soil) could all glean something from the fields and their manure helped to restore the fertility of the soil.

The 'hillfort' question: defensive works or social statements?
If domestic life revolved around farmsteads, what purpose did the hill enclosure serve? Were they refuges where people and stock would gather in times of crisis? Were they the sites of trade and exchange, religious foci or residences occupied by a powerful warrior aristocracy? Generally, hill enclosures have been divided into three main categories, of which the most common is the contour enclosure, one whose banks follows the contours around the crest of a hill. A second type is known as a cross-defence. This design is based partly on a rampart and ditch construction but is cut and defended on one side by a promontory. The third type, promontory hill enclosures or cliff castles, are designed on the principle that at least one or more slopes are so steep that ramparts need not be built. In Breconshire, all types are represented. They comprise a system of one (univallate) or more (multivallate) earth and stone banks and associated ditches enclosing an internal area, the size of which varies according partly to the size and shape of the hill top on which the enclosure is built and partly upon the type and intensity of use. The stone banks or earthen ramparts would have supported in most cases a timber palisade. Categories include a rear timber facing type (a single timber palisade standing vertically against a rampart), a box-style rampart (wooden palisade structure encasing the rampart), a box-style rampart incorporated into a sloping bank with timber lacing and a stone wall with timber laced supports.

A.H. Williams (1941) makes no distinction in terms of function, stating that: 'The different tribes lived for the most part in hillforts distributed far and wide throughout the country'. Cunliffe (1978) develops more refined ideas relating the role of enclosures to the societies in which they evolved. Although not an Iron Age innovation, the hill enclosure reached new heights of sophistication during this period. At the same time, society itself was becoming increasingly complex. A surge in the output of metalwork early in the first millennium BC suggests the importance of industrial production and also an emerging tribal class structure. By the end of the period, distinct tribal groupings were recognised by Greek and Roman writers, who also identified certain prominent individuals. Cunliffe argues that a more aggressive society was gradually emerging, one in which the amassing of large herds became increasingly important, both socially and economically. This, in turn, encouraged raiding. 'The direction in which society was developing during the latter part of the first millennium was towards active aggression and away from local self-protection. Social groups were polarising around individuals many of whom would have served principally as war leaders, not just as local kings,' (Cunliffe 1971:64). Similarly, the development of the hill enclosure, from simple beginnings to an often elaborate arrangement of defences and gateways, suggests '... power was passing into the hands of individuals at the expense of communal organisation. Put another way, the process of enclosure in the period c.600-400 is consistent with the emergence of a powerful aristocracy,' (ibid. 59).

It is true that the existence of permanent walled settlements suggests aggression on a significant scale, an increase in conflict perhaps resulting from climatic deterioration and ensuing competition for prime land. However, the extent to which violence and bloodshed were endemic at this time is questionable. A row of skulls found among burnt timbers at Bredon Hill, Worcestershire, could be taken as clear evidence of Celtic warfare. Equally, the Romans might have been responsible. It is true that the Celtic warrior enjoyed bragging about his heroic accomplishments. One early source comments: 'The Celts have in their company ... companions [who] pronounce their praises before the whole assembly and before each of the chieftains in turn as they listen.'

Enemies were reviled with equal relish. But this is verbal aggression—a war of words. Like the modern football 'supporter', the Celtic warrior would have used a whole range of verbal and visual devices to overawe his opponents. War cries and abuse, lamentation and chanting, ritual nakedness, body piercing and tattooing—all of these stop short of physical contact with the enemy. Actual conflict prior to the Roman conquest may well have amounted to little more than elaborate posturing on the part of a few prominent individuals—in other words, warfare may have been largely symbolic. As the archaeologist Stuart Piggott has observed: 'Within this framework of warfare, conducted on a petty scale ... fit the practices of individual combat, ritual nakedness in battle, head-hunting, battle-cries and chants, and the rest of the excitements dear to the simple heart of the hero,' (Piggott 1975:40).

The anthropological evidence tends to support such a view. In the Central Highlands of Papua New Guinea, for example, opposing sides in any conflict set out to maim rather than to kill so that tribal numbers are not depleted. Hunter/gatherer rock paintings from the Spanish Levant (the east coast of Spain from Barcelona to Cadiz) and North Africa (the Tassili-n-Ajjer massif in southern Algeria) present a similar story. Many frescoes portray warring archers with elaborate head-dresses in pitched battle, but the artist does not show any dead or wounded warriors. Indeed, on a number of panels the artist suggests execution and gladiatorial combat were the main mechanism for solving disputes. More recently, in the Trobriand Islands, west of Papua New Guinea, 19th-century missionaries introduced 'Trobriand cricket' as a means of settling such disputes, and the game is still used in this way today. Similarly, among the Celts there may well have been a discrepancy between the ideals of warring and the reality. This obviously presents problems for the conventional interpretation of hillforts as defensive works and the traditional characterisation of Celts as a bloodthirsty and warring people. It may only have been during the invasion period that mass slaughter became a reality.

The hillfort as an expression of territorial identity

Given this background of symbolic warfare, it can be seen that the term 'hillfort' suggests a militaristic function that is probably inaccurate for much, if not most, of the Iron Age. The literature portrays a society embroiled in warfare and political turmoil. However, although the massive earthworks suggest a world in which warfare was rife, we would prefer to play down the military role of the hill enclosure. There was no need to defend against large-scale, organised assault, as warfare at this time never amounted to more than limited skirmishing, possibly in the open areas between hill enclosures, and more often than not involving nothing more aggressive than threatening gestures and verbal abuse. We suggest the people who built these enclosures used a limited repertoire of basic architectural forms to serve a variety of purposes, arising from the political, economic and strategic needs of individual élites. In addition, the likelihood that the function of hill enclosures changed over time, perhaps as society became more complex during the centuries leading up to the expansion of Rome has to be considered. Generally the trend is from simple ramparts and entrances towards greater design complexity. Hill enclosures also tend to increase in size, although some contracted during the latter part of the Iron Age. In parts of southern Britain, hill enclosures were abandoned altogether, while others continued to evolve towards the status of true central places, possibly serving expanded territories as storage, administrative and craft production centres. There seems to be little evidence for this in south-east Wales.

The effort needed to construct the hillforts suggests the existence of a structure of authority able to mobilise and co-ordinate labour. Given their monumental scale, it is reasonable to suggest that hill enclosures were the most significant structures within the Iron Age landscape, the upper end of a hierarchy of sites that included farmsteads and coastal/estuarine settlements; the latter generally regarded as ephemeral features within the landscape. Although people may have made their home within the walls and traded cattle or other commodities with neighbouring groups, building a hill enclosure was essentially a symbolic act, a statement, a means of stamping authority on the landscape.

It may only have been during the 'national emergency' of the Roman invasion that hill enclosures served any real military/strategic need. When the Romans extended their imperial ambitions into north-west Europe, they encountered many 'barbaric' peoples. Among the most ferocious were the Silures, who occupied much of present-day Breconshire and who launched a violent campaign against the Romans. Yet it must be considered that the descriptions which the Romans have left us will be coloured by their own prejudices, whilst individual commanders would have exaggerated the strength of their enemies in order to enhance their own military prestige. The invasion period was a time of enormous instability and threat and it was this unprecedented situation that probably stimulated the formation of vast tribal domains, which probably coalesced out of a number of much smaller social groups. In this respect, tribal Britain was probably very like tribal Africa. For several decades it has been recognised that tribal labels have tended to be applied uncritically. The question was raised in the 1970s when Fried argued (1975) that the term 'tribe' was little more than a relic of colonial times, and that what were assumed to be tribes, in the sense of discrete ethnic groups whose members shared a common language and a sense of common identity, were in fact separate communities and dialect groups. It was only under the influence of western expansion that tribal domains emerged. The same may hold true for the invasion period, when indigenous groups were for the first time confronted by a campaign of organised subjugation. Roman expansion, like the European penetration of Africa and North America during the colonial era, threatened to tear apart the fabric of traditional society, and indeed ultimately succeeded in doing so. Indigenous forms of conflict could not have prepared native peoples for the scale and ferocity of Roman aggression and only by forging alliances could effective resistance be mounted. Prior to this 'national emergency' the picture is unclear. Hogg underlines the need for caution when he says: 'Tribal locations are seldom known before the Roman period, and their boundaries usually have an uncertainty of 30 or 40km at least,' (Hogg 1975:39). In earlier times, territories would probably have been much more compact, each taking one or more hill enclosure as its focus. The Roman invasion over-rode these territorial considerations, promoting a wider 'Celtic' identity. In the face of a formidable enemy, leaders of extraordinary qualities, such as Caratacus, emerged to weld clans together in uneasy alliance. Had the invasion never occurred, he, and others like him, would have remained small-time local chieftains, engaged in petty tit-for-tat skirmishes.

However, it should not be forgotten that the Mediterranean world probably began to impinge upon the societies of north-west Europe long before the Romans marched north. It has been said of America that, '... [European contact] had begun to transform the native cultures of North America long before any significant amount of information was recorded about them. These changes altered societies hundreds of miles inland from the frontiers of actual European settlement and affected every aspect of Indian life,' (Trigger 1982:6). The archaeological evidence for earlier Iron Age contact exchange, in particular from the 3rd and 4th century onwards, is concentrated mainly in the west of Britain. This exchange network emanated from the Mediterranean, using Brittany and the tribal group known as the Veneti to move luxury goods such as amphorae, metal work, pottery and limited coinage from south to north, although coinage arguably did not enter Britain until the 1st century BC. Nevertheless, the existence of trade with this part of Britain indicates the importance of tribal groups in Wales and south-west England. The fortunes of these areas changed dramatically during the mid-1st century, when the economic and political focus shifted to the south-east and intense trading alliances emerged between south-east British tribal groups and the Gallo-Belgic area. As a result, Haselgrove (1986) suggests that by the 1st century there were three settlement zones in southern Britain: the core, peripheral and outer zones, the latter including most of western Britain.

Pen-y-Crug

© CPAT

Hillfort/enclosure
Location: 3km north-west of Brecon (SO 029 304)
Access: Crossed by public paths

This substantial hill enclosure lies approximately 3km north-west of Brecon. From the town, take the B4520 towards Builth Wells. Take the first left turning along a country lane. From the track, Pen-y-Crug is clearly visible. Alternatively, one can walk from Brecon, past Pencrug Farm to the hill enclosure (walking distance is approximately 2km).

Located on marginal land in the centre of the county, this oval-shaped, multivallate enclosure lies 2km north-west of the confluence of the Usk and Honddu and may have been one of the most important centres in the area during the later Iron Age. Unfortunately, the structure has suffered damage from quarrying on the north, south and eastern sections.

Rising to a height of 331m OD, the 1.90ha hill enclosure measures 182m (north/south) x 134m (east/west) and occupies a

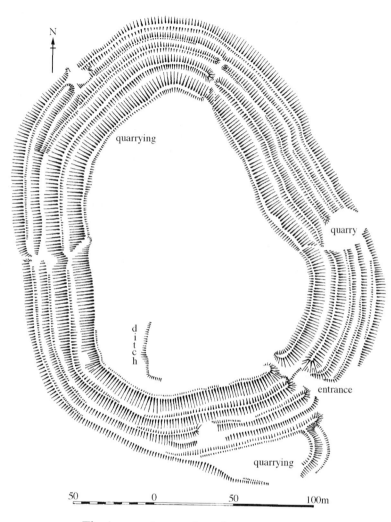

quarrying

quarry

ditch

entrance

quarrying

50   0   50   100m

The impressive earthworks at Pen-y-crug

conspicuous location, its earth and stone defences hugging the
contours of the hill. Four bracken-covered earth and stone ramparts
are visible for much of the circuit, with three on the west. These
were probably constructed using the 'downward construction' tech-
nique (Harding 1974), with material from the upper ditch being
used to form the lower rampart. On the south-east, the ramparts turn
inwards to form a simple funnel entrance. Although the enclosure

Looking south and towards Brecon (© CPAT)

sits on a steep hill, a causeway runs up from the south-east. Also on the south-east lies a hollow which may be the remains of a structure, probably a hut. The interior space shows evidence of ploughing, as well as grazing. An annex on the south may be a later addition. On the basis of the construction techniques employed and the elaborate design, the site has been interpreted as an important settlement, possibly having a 'focal administrative function' (RCAHM[W] 1986:16).

Approximately 2km to the south-west is Coed Fenni-fach Camp, a small single bank-and-ditch enclosure at 290m OD and extending over some 0.90ha. It is likely that this small enclosure, separated from Pen y Crug by a small tributary of the river Usk, was politically and economically related to the larger site.

Slwch Tump

Hillfort/enclosure
On the south-east edge of Brecon (SO 056 284)
Access: Via a public path from Brecon Hospital

To the south-east of Brecon, close to army barracks is Slwch Tump. The approach to this site is from the north-west, close to Brecon Hospital. From the hospital to the site the distance is about 0.3km and the site is clearly visible.

Like neighbouring Pen-y-Crug, this enclosure occupies a prominent hilltop site 248m OD, but, unlike the other smaller hillfort in the vicinity of Pen-y-Crug which is believed to have been subservient to Pen-y-Crug, Slwch Tump is probably of different function and possibly the earlier (RCAHM[W] 1986). The enclosure stands 1.3km east of the confluence of the Usk and Honddu, the Usk flowing south-east and the Honddu south, the rivers perhaps defining a territory associated with the enclosure. The univallate system of defences comprises a single earth and stone rampart standing 3m-4.6m high, together with traces of a ditch. The ramparts follow the natural contours of the hill, hence the irregular shape. A series of post-medieval banks follow the line of the inner rampart. Theophilus Jones, in his 1809 *History of the County of Brecknock*, mentions 'a double foss, in some places nearly

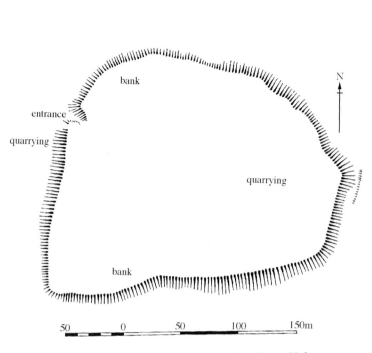

bank

entrance

quarrying

quarrying

bank

N

| 50 | 0 | 50 | 100 | 150m |

Slwch Tump, overlooking the River Usk

destroyed'. To the north-west is a simple inturned entrance, the southern part of which has been quarried away. It has been suggested that Slwch Tump once supported a large population, serving as a focus for economic and political control and, with Allt yr Esgair and Myarth, may have formed a contemporary line of forts along the Usk Valley (RCAHM[W] 1986). However, a combination of ploughing and internal quarrying has robbed posterity of much potential evidence.

An estate map dated 1781 records that the fort lay within a field named Ginger Wall.

Twyn Llechfaen

© CPAT

Univallate hillfort/enclosure
Location: 1km north of Llechfaen (SO 082 291)
Access: Can be reached from public footpaths

Go to Lower Farm, north of Llechfaen (itself east of Brecon), and follow a footpath east from the farm. Approximately 300m along the path take another path north and proceed for 500m. The fort is on top of the hill, approximately 150m west of the path.

This small univallate hillfort standing 319m OD on the summit of a prominent hill lies approximately 1.5km north of the Usk and 1km east of the Afon Brynych. To the north, the land rises to more than 300m OD. There are no other enclosures in the immediate vicinity, nor any springs or tributaries. The site has yielded pottery of 3rd or 4th century BC date (including a single sherd assigned to Malvernian stamped ware) and the remains of ox, sheep and pig. The ramparts, constructed from dumps of clay revetted and capped with sandstone blocks, form a triangle enclosing an area of some 0.37ha, with an entrance at the south. The remains of a possible oval lean-to just west of the entrance included a post hole and a deposit containing coarse pottery, slingstones and animal bones. A small flag-paved floor towards the centre of the enclosure yielded, in addition, an unidentifiable iron object. The excavator, Hubert

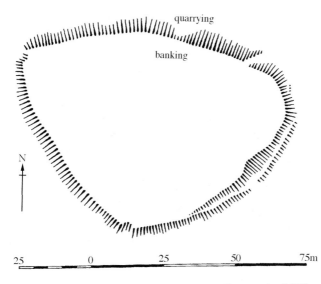

Twyn Llechfaen, excavated by H.N. Savory in 1959

Savory, who dug trenches in 1959 to reveal the construction of the defences which revealed that the enclosure bank was considerably more substantial than at present, possibly exceeding 5m in height, believed the animal remains—three oxen, nine sheep and four pigs—gave a fair indication of the relative importance of these species.

The interior has been ploughed in the past and the rampart has been reduced to form a 'talus' slope which is partially masked by shrubs. The modern field layout follows the interior lines of the ramparts.

Hillis Fort

Hillfort/enclosure
Location: 4km west of Bronllys (SO 114 327)
Access: Crossed by footpaths

The Hillis enclosure (also known as Llanfilo Camp) is located approximately 4km west of the village of Bronllys, close to the A438. From Bronllys, along the main road, take a left turn signposted 'Llanfilo'. The Hillis enclosure is clearly visible to the west of the village. There are several footpaths which lead to the enclosure (distance is approximately 0.5km).

This is one of three large enclosures dominating and controlling the hinterlands of the Black Mountains. Located on Hillis Hill 310m OD, the site has commanding views over the Afon Dulas and Afon Lynfi. At present, most of the defences are wooded. Indeed, along the crest of the scarp there is a line of trees. Oval in shape, it measures 330m on its north-south axis and 130m east-west. The

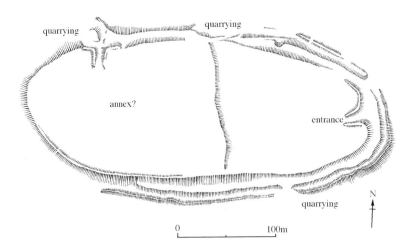

Hillis hill enclosure with possible annex

enclosure follows the natural contours of the hill. Towards the western part of the interior the land rises to its highest point, represented by a triangulation point. Two ramparts, visible on the south and west and rising to approximately 1.8m, enclose an area of 3.6ha, and comprise consolidated stone rubble (RCAHM[W] 1986:106). The most complex entrance (one of two) lies on the north-west, where a 24m-passageway, again affected by quarrying, narrows as it extends into the interior. Towards the outer part of the entrance there is evidence of rock cutting, which may have created a more imposing structure. This entrance may have led to a substantial causeway running close to the line of the northern defences, but unfortunately quarrying has destroyed all traces of the area where the outer entrance and causeway met. To the south is a deeply inturned entrance. Interestingly, this appears to be the entrance for cattle (assuming half the hill enclosure was used as a corral) and the more complex of the two for people (assuming the enclosure was settled, either permanently or periodically). The complex entrance, together with a substantial causeway, suggest the builders of the enclosure were intending to construct something truly impressive. The ramparts are weakest at the north and there are no clear defences on part of the eastern side (Houlder 1978:126), probably as a result of agricultural activity. There is evidence of a small bank running through the middle of the enclosure, which may have divided the domestic space from a corralling area. Heavy ploughing of the interior has led to erosion of the shallow soils. Quarrying is evident around the north-eastern part of the enclosure and also on the northern rampart closest to the bisecting bank, where part of the northern defences have been destroyed.

This substantial site, with its large sub-divided interior and two entrances, one of which is complex, typifies many of the larger Welsh enclosures. Within 2km to the south of Hillis are three smaller univallate enclosures which probably acted as satellites (Children & Nash 1996). Equidistant to the north and south are two rivers flowing east-west, the Afon Dulas to the north, and Afon Gwlithen to the south, suggesting that Hillis and its satellites were enclosed within a series of natural boundaries.

The size of the corralling area at Hillis suggests an emphasis on the ownership of cattle.

Y Gaer

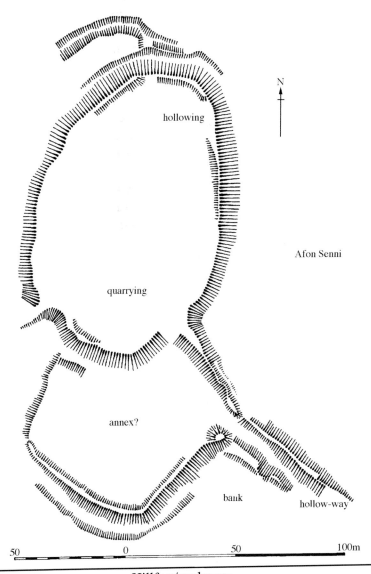

Hillfort/enclosure
Location: 2.5km south of Sennybridge (SN 922 263)
Access: Located off the Heol Cefn-y-gaer footpath, south of Defynnog

This hill enclosure, one of only a handful within the western part of Breconshire, lies approximately 2.5km south of the village of Sennybridge. From the A40 to the west of the town, take the A4067 signposted 'Swansea'. At the small hamlet of Defynnog take the first left across the Afon Senni. Y Gaer is located approximately 300m south-west of this small country track. The site is enclosed by woodland and therefore difficult to find, but stands on the highest point within the immediate landscape.

This enclosure, located centrally between the Afon Senni to the east and the Cwm Treweren, stands 345m OD and consists of an oval univallate rampart with a later sub-rectangular annex. A holloway approaches the annex on the south-eastern side and may have been the original causeway. Although rare in Wales, enclosures with annexes do sometimes occur, especially in the Marches, *e.g.* Little Doward and Croft Ambrey, but only where there is surplus land close to or adjacent to the main enclosure. It may be that annexes supersede the banks that sometimes divide the interior space of enclosures. On the south-eastern rampart of the annex, the entrance appears to be inturned, creating a small promontory possibly forming part of a substantial gateway. Where the annex meets the main enclosure, the rampart has been extended to block the entrance, so there is no 'official' entrance in the main enclosure.

Y Gaer sits on a natural ridge with fairly steep sides. The interior is flat, although there is evidence of quarrying having left exposed crags in the southern section of the main interior. The enclosure measures approximately 115m x 80m and encompasses an area of about 0.8ha. Although the main enclosure is heavily eroded, the annex is in better condition and measures 70m square and has an interior area of 0.33ha. Running from the northern part of the outer rampart is a further small enclosure, referred to as a 'toe', with no bank or ditch on the south-western side. The function of this feature is unclear. The annex itself, like other such structures in this part of Wales, probably served as a cattle corral. To the east and south-east of both the enclosure and annex is an old ridgeway track known as Heol Cefn-y-gaer, which appears to cross over the older holloway leading to the annex.

Twyn-y-Gaer

© CPAT

Hillfort/enclosure
Location: Near the A40, 5km to the west of Brecon (SN 990 281)
Access: A public footpath runs to the south-east of the enclosure,
whilst other tracks lead to it

Approximately 5km west of Brecon along the A40, take a left turn
signposted 'Llanspyddid'—Twyn-y-Gaer is visible from both the
main road and this small country lane. Approximately 1.5km down
this lane is a series of rough tracks located on the left. About 100m
up either of these tracks is the enclosure. It is worth noting that also
close by are the remains of a Roman road known as Sarn Helen, and
a castle mound.

This oval hill enclosure located south of the Usk and north of the
Afon Tarell consists of a single bank and entrance. There is
evidence of quarrying and recent agricultural use within the interior. Dug into the rampart on the north-eastern side is the remains
of a possible sub-rectangular hut, possibly medieval in date.
Outside the enclosure and within the same direction as the hut are
several pillow mounds which probably date to either the medieval
or early post-medieval periods.

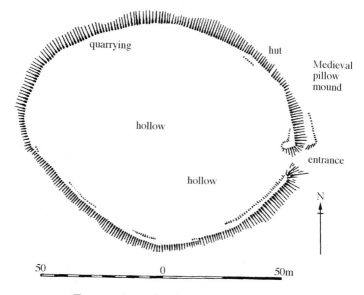

Twyn y Gaer overlooking the river Usk

Twyn-y-Gaer is located on a rounded hill top, 360m OD and is close to a small enclosure known as St Illtyd's churchyard (SN 971 261) 1.8km south-west of the hill enclosure, which has been used since the 19th century as a graveyard and surrounds a small chapel. The site stands about 340m OD, measures 112m (east-west) x 87m (north-south) and has an area of 0.55ha. On the north and east sides of the enclosure are many tributaries running into the Usk. The entrance, simple in construction, is slightly inturned on the northern section, outside of which there appears to be a secondary bank which may form part of the entrance complex.

Corn-y-Fan

© CPAT

Hillfort/enclosure
Location: Between Brecon and Builth Wells (SN 985 354)
Access: Public access

From Brecon, take the B4520 north towards Builth Wells. Approximately 8km up this road take a left turn to Merthyr Cynog. Proceed past the church towards the Afon Yscir-Fechan. Immediately across the bridge take the first left and proceed down this track for about 1.5km (following the line of the river). Corn-y-Fan is located within woodland, approximately 100m east of the Afon Yscir-Fechan.

This hill enclosure, consisting of a triple bank-and-ditch system, has been classified as a promontory hillfort and stands approximately 350m OD. Located on the highest point within the immediate landscape, Corn-y-Fan overlooks the Afon Ysgir Fechan and the Afon Ysgir Fawr to the north-west; both tributaries running into the Afon Ysgir to the south-east. The triple bank and ditch system,

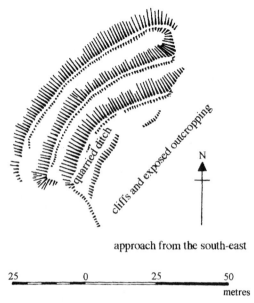

approach from the south-east

25   0   25   50
metres

Promontory hill enclosure of Corn-y-Fan

which is well preserved and visible from a long distance, encloses a small area of land measuring 55m x 20m, a total area of 0.1ha. To the south-east the banks fall away to steep cliffs and the approaches would have been from either the north or the north-east. The truly monumental rampart and ditches are similar in form to many other promontory enclosures on both sides of the Bristol Channel, such as Sudbrook Camp. At the foot of the third ditch there appears to have been some quarrying while on top of the enclosure the area has been subjected to ploughing. Between each rampart the ditches measure approximately 10m wide and on either side, to the south-west and north-east, the ramparts curl towards the south-east. The banks stand 4m high. According to Harding (1974:362-64) this enclosure appears to have been constructed by throwing the soil from the ditch onto the ground on the upper side. The RCAHM(W) inventory (1986:42) suggested that this enclosure or what they call a hillfort is poorly defended. However, we would suggest that this hill enclosure is not a defensive structure but merely one for visual display.

Crug Hywel

© CPAT

Hillfort/enclosure
Location: On the flanks of the Black Mountains above
Crickhowell (SO 225 206)
Access: Can be reached across the open mountainside

This enclosure, one of the most dramatic locations in Breconshire, is close to Table Mountain and overlooks the town of Crickhowell. From the town, proceed north along a country track signposted Llanbedr. Around 2km and on the left hand side is Crug Hywel. Along this road are a number of footpaths leading to this site and Pen Cerrig Calch beyond. This area is open mountain and moorland and extreme caution should be taken.

This monument, a multivallate enclosure standing at approximately 450m above sea level, is pear-shaped in design, measuring 162m from north-west to south-east by 59m and encompasses an area of 0.63ha, with an entrance on the eastern flank (RCAHM[W] 1986:119). On all sides except that to the north the land falls away steeply towards the fertile valleys of the Usk to the south-west and Grwyne Fechan to the south-east. The enclosure appears to be strategically placed at the point where at least seven small tributaries rise. Around the edge of the defences are the remains of a stone wall which in places has become a stone bank and to the south-east a turfed bank. The entrance appears to have some elaboration which is focused around the inner rampart and is approached by a track running from the north that follows the contour of the lower scarp slopes. On either side there are small raised platforms which curl in to the inner rampart which may be sentry posts.

Within the interior are four shallow depressions located on the eastern and western flanks which lie against the inner rampart, which may represent hut circles. Each of the depressions are quite substantial measuring up to 11m x 11m, and any structure of such a size would have supported an extended family consisting of maybe 10-15 individuals. With a minimum of four such houses, the community using this hill enclosure would have been quite substantial. Interestingly, the hut depressions are grouped in pairs and within these two groups one hut depression is bigger than the other. Furthermore, their location, against the inner ramparts, suggests both protection from the prevailing easterly and westerly winds as well as reducing the building time by utilising the inner rampart wall as one of the walls for the hut. It could be the case that a building of this size and located at this altitude could not survive as a free-standing structure. To the south-east of the hill enclosure approximately 100m down slope is a small bank and wall which may be associated with this monument.

Coed Pen-Twyn

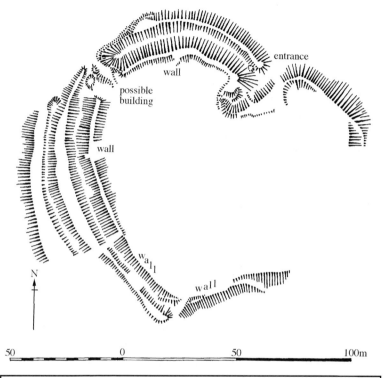

entrance

wall

possible
building

wall

wall

wall

N

50   0   50   100m

| Hillfort/enclosure |
| Location: 2km south-west of Crickhowell (SO 193 162) |
| Access: On private land |

This enclosure lies close to Mynydd Llangattock approximately
2km south-west of Crickhowell, within an area of limestone quarrying. From Llangattock, across the River Usk from Crickhowell,
take a small country lane signposted 'Penrhiw'. About 1km along
this road and close to dramatic uplands to the south, is Coed Pen-
Twyn. Its name suggests that this site is located within woodland,
which, at present, it is.

This enclosure, a large elliptical bivallate structure, is located
south of the Nant Onnau and north of the summit of Craig Y Cilau.
Above this enclosure is an impressive cliff face which overlooks

the Cwm Onneu Fach. Above the cliffs is a glacial lake known as Pwll Gwy-rhoc. Standing 307m OD, this enclosure has a series of impressive earthworks, although the interior and some of the ramparts have been subjected to ploughing and tree-planting. Some of the ramparts have also suffered from denudation. The bivallate series of ramparts and ditches are located on the west part of the enclosure. There appear to be two entrances, both of which are complex in structure. Surrounding the inner bank is a series of later drystone walls which act as field systems, both within and outside the hill enclosure, whilst on the north-eastern outer rampart and abutting the outer face is the remains of a small cottage, possibly belonging to a shepherd. The internal space measures 140m (north-west) x 103m (south-east), an area of 0.9ha. The ramparts are constructed of stone with the highest being approximately 4.5m. At the south-east end, there are no remains of any banks or ditches; these appear to have been levelled in the historical past. According to the RCAHM(W) (1986:78) the western rampart and ditch system appears to have been strengthened but left unfinished. We would suggest, however, that this is the most intact part of the monument. The entrances are difficult to discern in that they may have been cut at a later date, and that within the north-east section of the enclo-sure has a series of inturned banks and ditches with a bank blocking the central section of the entrance. Movement through this entrance would be hampered by the small bank. The area around this entrance has been subjected to modifications in more recent times in the form of drystone walls and a series of paths. In the north-western section of the enclosure is a narrower entrance which has well defined sides. Within the western wall is the site of a possible hut—a hollow, approximately 11m in diameter. This impressive hill enclosure interestingly does not have any nearby hill Iron Age monuments.

The Gaer

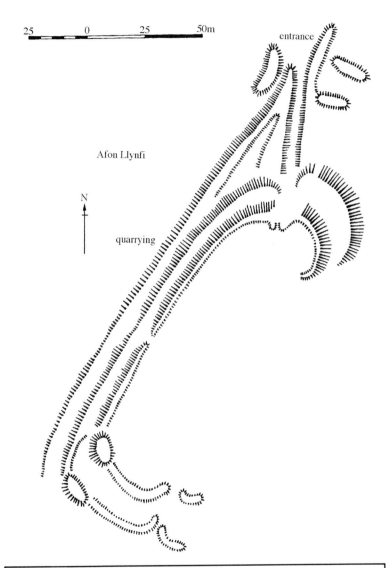

Hillfort/enclosure
Location: Three Cocks, near Glasbury (SO 175 376)
Access: On private land, and hidden by banks and railway lines

This site (also known as Gwernyfed Park) lies within the southern boundaries of the small village of Three Cocks, close to Glasbury. From the A438 still within the village take the turning to the south signposted 'Llanigon'. Both this site and a further enclosure are located approximately 50m from a cross-roads still within the village. Also west of the village is Little Lodge long barrow.

This small multivallate fort, rectangular in form, is located on a series of tributaries that flow into the Afon Llynfi 0.5km to the west. Beyond this is the north-western section of the river Wye. Located on a plateau, 150m OD, this enclosure was excavated by Herbert Savory in 1951. Unlike other enclosures within the county, The Gaer is not on the highest point in the immediate landscape but approximately 35m above the valley floor. In the recent past, the site has been levelled so much that very little of the banks and ditches in the north and west of the enclosure remain visible, whilst the interior has been subjected to ploughing which has damaged the inner ramparts. When in use, the triple bank and double ditch which faces the north-west part of the upper Wye Valley would have formed part of an impressive series of earthworks. To the north-east and south-east the double bank and ditch systems curl in and enclose the interior. The site is enclosed by a small stream which runs south-west/north-east into one of the tributaries of the Afon Llynfi. The interior space has an area of 0.44ha and measures 125m (north-east/south-west) by 47m. To the south-west and north-east the enclosure has bivallate earthworks, whilst to the north-east there is an entrance and an enclosed causeway which cuts into the bedrock. From the entrance to the causeway measures around 60m. According to the RCAHM(W) (1986), within the east section outside the bivallate earthworks is a possible annex.

Savory's 1951 excavation concentrated mainly on the ramparts east of the north-east entrance. He concluded, perhaps unsurprisingly, that the ramparts were constructed from the material dug out from the ditches, each rampart being constructed of different material which was dependent on how deep the construction trenches were dug. Savory also noted that the V-shaped ditches had been infilled with stone, amongst which were so-called sling stones, as well as a single sherd of Romano-British pottery. Within the bottom fill of the inner ditch was clay up to 0.4m deep which contained late Neolithic flint and an early Iron Age potsherd as well as flecks of charcoal. It is probable that this ditch fill is the result of solifluction. The outer ditch measures 4m wide and 2.1m deep. The upper deposits within both ditches appeared to be soil gradually accumulated from the banks as they weathered. Excavation of the entrance revealed that the passage to the interior measured only 1.07m wide. On either side of the entrance before the inner ditch was a series of post holes which may represent a gate structure, whilst on the west side was evidence of a sandstone revetment wall which abuts part of the rampart. The location of the two post holes and a further two post holes some 3m into the entrance has been suggested by Savory as representing mooring posts belonging to a retractable bridge that would have spanned the width of the inner ditch.

Approximately 200m north-east of The Gaer is a hill enclosure known as Small Gaer, which may have acted as a satellite to this enclosure. This site is severely eroded and its origins are questionable.

Castell Dinas

© CPAT

Hillfort/enclosure adapted for medieval castle use
Location: 4km south of Talgarth (SO 179 301)
Access: Reached by public paths

This impressive enclosure lies south of Talgarth and close to the
Neolithic monuments of Ty Isaf and Cwm Fforest. From Talgarth
take the A479 south towards Crickhowell. Approximately 4km

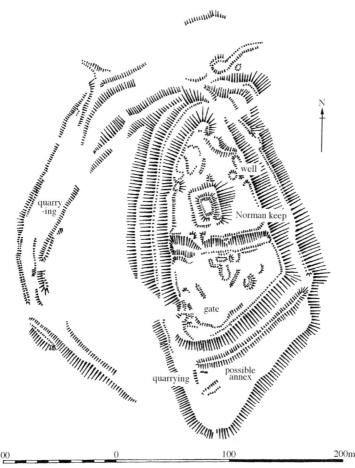

Castell Dinas, an Iron Age enclosure with Norman castle in the centre of the site

along this road, take a left turn signposted Ty Isaf. The enclosure is visible both from the main road and the country lane. Along the road are several footpaths leading to the site (walking distance approximately half a kilometre).

This hill enclosure is one of the most complex of its kind in the county. Mainly oval in shape and multivallate in design it is located on the summit of a steep-sided hill. Located at 450m OD and with extensive views to the south and west, this hill enclosure has also been used during the early medieval period for a castle site. Unlike other hill enclosures within the area Castell Dinas stands alone; there are no known satellite enclosures close by. It is surrounded by many tributaries, two in particular—the Afon Rhiangoll and Afon Ennig—may delineate some form of territoriality. The complex form of this enclosure, now consisting of a series of grassed stone banks, appears to be designed similarly to other large enclosures within the county. Measuring 174m (north-south) x 93m (east-west) and enclosing an area of 1.03ha, the earlier features of the enclosure have been incorporated into or removed by the medieval castle. Furthermore to the south-west and to the west many of the outer banks and ditches have been subjected to extensive quarrying. Within the interior the hill enclosure appears to be divided into three sections. The inner rampart encloses two of these sections and is typical of hill enclosures in this area in that there appears to be a domestic area and a corralling area. To the south is the third section which appears to be attached to the main hill enclosure proper, and is arguably part of the enclosure line. It appears that the central enclosure was bisected at some point to create two enclosures. The original outer scarp of the inner rampart is approximately 6m in height, but has been added to during the medieval period when the castle was in use. The medieval castle, rectangular in plan, is located in the northern enclosure. Close by, to the north-east of the castle, is a well which would have probably been used during the Iron Age and two further wells are located outside the main perimeter to the north and to the north-west. There are two entrances similar to Hillis: one in the north and the other in the south. The most probable entrance of Iron Age date is that in the north where the land gently slopes away, and it is probable that some form of causeway led to this entrance. The entrance appears to have been rather complex at one point and it could be the case that it was used by settlers rather than cattle. To the south there is a smaller and less impressive entrance and due to the intense medieval activity in this area it is difficult to discern whether this is of Iron Age date. To the west of the main ramparts is a series of outer banks and ditches which appear to delineate an outer enclosure and may be a funnel-like causeway leading to the north entrance. However, due to successive ploughing regimes, quarrying and tree planting, these structures have become fragmented and are difficult to discern.

Allt yr Esgair

Hillfort/enclosure
Location: South of Llangorse Lake (SO 127 243)
Access: Public footpath

This impressive enclosure lies just south of Llangorse Lake. From Brecon take the A40 south towards Crickhowell. Just before the village of Bwlch is a left turning signposted 'Llangasty-Talyllyn'. Approximately 20m from this turning is a footpath leading to the summit of Allt yr Esgair, walking distance 2km. Incidentally, this track is also apart of the Roman road which runs from Brecon to Bwlch.

This extremely large elongated enclosure, which follows the contours of a prominent ridge known as Allt yr Esgair, stands 395m OD and is equidistant between the rivers Usk and Llynfi. This hill enclosure has steep natural defences on all sides with prominent cliffs along the western edge. Because of this, the only safe way to approach with cattle would have been from the south along the spine of the hill. Over the past, this enclosure has been subjected to forest planting and linear quarrying, with the result that much of the central section of the enclosure has been damaged and the original hillfort plan confused, whilst the balance is covered by bracken. Running up the side of the hill and also within the interior is a series

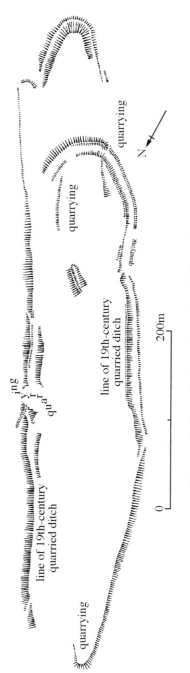

The much disturbed earthworks of Allt yr Esgair

quarrying

quarrying

quarrying

quarrying

line of 19th-century
quarried ditch

line of 19th-century
quarried ditch

quarrying

quarrying

200m

0

N

of drystone walls which probably date from the medieval and post-medieval periods. The enclosure measures 566m north/south by 115m east/west and covers an area of 5.45ha. The enclosure appears to have been built in two phases, and at the southern end the original line of the ramparts appears to be 400m shorter than the southern extent of a double bank and ditch. Quarrying on the original line and cutting into what we term a secondary phase of building has hampered any interpretation, but it is possible that the earlier line of the southern extent of the enclosure is marked by the southernmost bank and ditch formation because the western line of this feature appears to go underneath and into the interior of the hill enclosure proper. To the south-east of the outer bank and ditch formation is a possible entrance to this section of the hill enclosure. There is a further opening between this and the interior proper which runs along the eastern inner rampart. Within the central part of the interior, east of the main quarrying area, there is evidence of a double rampart and ditch system which is interesting because this is also the steepest side; it would seem more appropriate to construct multivallate ramparts on the north-west flank where the slope is less steep. To the north-west is the best preserved section of the defences and it appears that a simple inturned entrance was located within the northern part of the enclosure. Unlike many of the larger enclosures in this area there appears to be no segregating bank and no substantial entrances. It could be that this enclosure was merely used for stock rearing, for it is certainly located near fertile land rather than within a marginal area.

To the west of Allt yr Esgair and 30m below the summit is a small enclosure, Llansanffraid, possibly a staging post for corralled stock and perhaps acting as a satellite to the main hill enclosure. It measures roughly 50m by 30m with an entrance to the north-west.

Appendix I
Scheduled Ancient Monuments (SAMS) by Parish

Note: Within the counties of England and Wales, the Secretary of State has seen fit to protect archaeological sites which deserve statutory protection. 'Under Section I of the Ancient Monuments and Archaeological Areas Act 1979, the Secrtary of State is required to compile, for the purposes of the 1979 Act, a statutory schedule of monuments which appear to be of national importance. The Secretary of State has concluded that the monuments described [in this case Breconshire] in the attached schedule are monuments of national importance, and they have been included in the statutory Schedule'. The following sites are scheduled according to the following criteria: period, rarity, documentation, group value, survival/condition, fragility/vulnerability, diversity and potential. The schedule clearly states, under Section 42 of the same Act, that the use of metal detectors on any archaeological or historical site is an offence. Listed below are sites which have statutory protection.

Parish	CADW Ref. No.	Monument Name	Grid. Ref.	Monument Type and Period
Brecon	17/20449/BR038(POW)	Slwch Camp	SO 043 288	HE/IA
Bronllys	17/1879/BR029(POW)	Pipton	SO 160 373	LCTIN
Bronllys	17/1554/BR048(POW)	Bronllys	SO 131 377	RB/BA
Bronllys	1711878/BR079(POW)	Bronllys	SO 168 381	RB/BA
Bronllys	17/1553/BR085(POW)	Llyswen Camp	SO 128 379	HE/IA
Bronllys	17/1552/BR0S6(POW)	Llangoed Wood	SO 123 396	SS/BA
Cilmery	17/2256/BR147(POW)	Tower Hill	SN 998 517	RB/BA
Cray	17/1129/BR035(POW)	Twyn-y-Gaer	SN 922 263	HE/IA
Crickhowell	17/1181/BROI6(POW)	Gwernvale	SO 211 192	LCT/N
Erwood	17/0790/BR033(POW)	Camp	SO 088 421	HE/IA
Erwood	1713170/BRI81(POW)	Waun Gunllwch	SO 061 411	RC/BA
Erwood	17/6521/BR204(POW)	Cefn Clawdd	SO 032 405	RC/BA
Erwood	1716520/BR205(POW)	Gwaun Ymryson	SO 032 411	RC/BA
Erwood	17/6513/BR206(POW)	Banc y Celyn	SO 052 463	SC/BA
Felin-fach	17/1350/BR039(POW)	Weston Camp	SO 110 327	HE/IA
Felin-fach	1711349/BR040(POW)	Llanfilo Camp	SO 113 328	HE/IA
Glantwymyn	1712641/MGI47(POW)	Rhos-dyrnog	SH 828 005	SS/BA
Glasbury	17/2448/RD128(POW)	Neuadd-Glan-Gwy	SO 127 412	SS/BA
Gwrnyfed	17/0683/BR067(POW)	Little lodge	SO 183 380	LCT/N
Gwrnyfed	17/2517/BR159(POW)	Gwernyfed Park	SO 175 376	HE/IA
Honddu Isaf	17/2149/BR034(POW)	Twyn-y-Gaer	SO 054 352	HE/IA
Llanafanfawr	17/2037/BR065(POW)	Saith-Maen	SN 949 603	SSIBA

Llanafanfawr	17/0695/BRO90(POW)	Capel Rhos	SN 948 558	SSIBA
Llanafanfawr	17/0696/BRO91(POW)	Dol-y-Felin	SN 976 550	SS/BA
Llanafanfawr	17/0982/BR095(POW)	Cam-y-Geifr	SN 971 604	RC/BA
Llanafanfawr	17/1827/BR096(POW)	Pen-Llys	SN 998 584	HE/IA
Llanafanfawr	17/0589/BR097(POW)	Cefn Ty-Mawr	SN 985 577	LCT/N
Llanafanfawr	17/0744BR098(POW)	Coed Ty-Mawr	SN 986 576	HE/IA
Llanfihangel	17/1684/BR059(POW)	Mynydd Llangorse	SO 166 261	RC/BA
Lianfihanget	1711334/BR112(POW)	Llwyn-y-Fedwen	SO 156 204	SSIBA
Llanfihangel	1711332/BR115(POW)	Coed y Gaer	SO 176 240	HEIIA
Llanfihangel	17/1335/BR1 16(POW)	Myarth Camp	SO 174 207	HEIIA
Llanfihangel	17/1331/BR124(POW)	Bwlch	SO 154 229	RC/BA
Llanfihangel	1710568/BR125(POW)	Cefn Moel	SO 156 237	RB/BA
Llanfihangel	17/0213/BR133(POW)	Penmyarth	SO 182 198	SS/BA
Llanfrynach	1712162/BR011(POW)	Ty Illytud	SO 098 264	LCT/N
Llanftynach	17/2259/BRI51(POW)	Coed y Caerau	SO 069 240	HE/IA
Llanfrynach	1712340/BR154(POW)	Plas-y-Gaer	SO 033 247	HE/IA
Llangamarch	17/2370/BRI00(POW)	Ffynnon RB	SN 925 431	RB/BA
Llangamarch	17/2369/BRI0I(POW)	Tri Chrugiau	SN 932 437	RB/BA
Llangainarch	17/2368/BRI02(POW)	Drover's Anns	SN 961 464	RB/BA
Llangattock	17/1143/BR028(POW)	Garn Coch	SO 212 177	LCT/N
Llangattock	17/10(WBRO60(POW)	Ffawyddog Gaer	SO 196 184	HE/IA
Llangattock	17/3644/BRI90(POW)	Coed Pentwyn	SO 193 162	HE/IA
LIangors	1711684/BR059(POW)	Mynydd Llangorse	SO 166 261	RC/BA
Llangors	1712261/BR]53(POW)	Allt yr Esgair	SO 124 248	HEIIA
Liangors	17/2518/BR158(POW)	Crannog	SO 128 269	PS/IA?
Lianigon	17/1872/BR0I2(POW)	Pen-y-Wyrlod	SO 224 398	LCT/N
Llanigon	1711425/BR I 19(POW)	Twyn-y-Boddau	SO 241 386	RB/BA
Llanigon	17/2693/BR167(POW)	Blaenau	SO 239 373	SC/BA
Llanwrthwl	17/0603/BR094(POW)	Banc Ystrdd-Wen	SN 981 615	RC/BA
Llanwrthwl	17/0982/BR095(POW)	Carn-y-Gelifr	SN 971 604	RC/BA
Llanwrthwl	17/3398/BRI84(POW)	Cryn-Fryn	SN 977 623	RC/BA
Llanwrthwl	17/6552/BR2OS(POW)	Esgair Ceiliog	SN 897 606	RC/BA
Llanwrthwl	17/6553/BR209(POW)	Craig y Llysiau	SN 885 612	HE/IA
Llanwrthwl	17/6554/BR210(POW)	Craig Rhiwnant	SN 882 613	SS/BA
Llanwrthwl	17/6555/BR211(POW)	Esgair Hafod	SN 891 606	RC/BA
Llanwrthwl	17/6571/BR212(POW)	y Gamriw	SN 943 614	RC/BA
Llanwrthwl	17/6573/BR213(POW)	y Gamriw	SN 953 617	RC/BA
Llanwrthwl	17/6574/BR214(POW)	Garn Lwyd	SN 919 618	RC/BA
Llanwrthwl	17/6572/BR217(POW)	Carnau Ccfn-y-Ffordd	SN 9-54 606	
				RC/SS/BA
Llanwrtyd Wells	17/151 I/BR132(POW)	Cambrian Factory	SN 885 474	SS/BA
Llywel	1712040/BR069(POW)	Mynydd Bach-Trecastell	SN 833 311	
				SC/BA
Llywel	17/1695/BR070(POW)	Nant Tarw	SN 819 258	SC/BA
Llywel	1710595BR071(POW)	Cerrig Duon	SN 851 206	SC/BA

Llywel	17/0344/BR142(POW)	Mynydd Bach-Trecastell	SN 830 309	RC/BA
Llywcl	17/0-145/BR144(POW)	Gwern-Wyddog	SN 833 283	SS/BA
Maescar	17/1571/BR0I7(POW)	Maen Llia	SN 924 191	SS/BA
Maescar	1710717/BR032(POW)	Clawdd British	SN 862 369	HE/IA
Maescar	171 66/BRI04(POW)	Gwar-y-Felin	SN 925 349	RC/BA
Maescar	17/2363/BRI07(POW)	Garn Wen	SN 877 368	RC/BA
Maescar	17/2362/BRI08(POW)	Bryn Melin	SN 889 369	RC/BA
Maescar	17/0346/BR143(POW)	Hirllwyn	SN 889 382	HE/IA
Maescar	17/2576/BR163(POW)	Maen Llia	SN 922 189	RB/BA
Maescar	17/6575/BR218(POW)	Dixies Corner	SN 870 366	HEIIA
Maescar	17/6570/BR219(POW)	Llyn Nant-Llys	SN 888 366	RB/BA
Merthyr Cy.	1710764/BR051(POW)	Corn y Fan	SN 985 354	HE/IA
Merthyr Cy.	17/1133/BR052(POW)	Gaer Fawr	SO 021 380	HE/IA
Merthyr Cy.	17/1132/BR053(POW)	Gaer Fach	SN 009 366	HEIIA
Merthyr Cy.	17/6523/BR202(POW)	Cornelau Uchaf	SO 029 403	HE/IA
Merthyr Cy.	17/6522/BR203(POW)	Twyn y Post	SO 028 409	RC/BA
Merthyr Cy.	1716527/BR207(POW)	Bailey Bach	SO 030 392	RC/C/BA
Talgarth	17/1067/BR002(POW)	Ffostyll	SO 179 348	LCT/N
Taigarth	1712163/BR006(POW)	Ty -Isaf	SO 182 290	LCT/N
Talgarth	1710809/BR007(POW)	Cwm Fforest	SO 183 295	LCTIN
Talgarth	17/1687/BR0I3(POW)	Mynydd Troed	SO 161 284	LCT/N
Talgarth	17/0538/BR0I5(POW)	Castell Dinas	SO 179 301	HEIIA
Talgarth	17/2064/BR062(POW)	Talgarth	SO 155 326	HE/IA
Talgarth	17/2065/BR129(POW)	Pen Trumau	SO 196 292	RC/BA
Talgarth	17/3121/BR175(POW)	Penywyrlod	SO 150 351	LCT/N
Talybont	17/2141/BR036(POW)	Tump Wood	SO 113 215	HEIIA
Talybont	1711233/BR123(POW)	Y Gaer, Dol-y-Gaer	SO 059 148	HEIIA
Talybont	17/0216/BRI40(POW)	Gilston	SO 117 237	SSIBA
Taiybont	1712261/BR153(POW)	Allt yr Esgair	SO 124 248	HEIIA
Talybont	17/3734/BR197(POW)	Alit yr Esgair	SO 123 242	HE/IA
Tawe-Uschaf	1712038/BR072(POW)	Saith Maen	SN 833 154	RC/BA
Vale of Grwyncy	17/6361/BRO61(POW)	Crickhowell	SO 228 186	HEIIA
Vale of Grwyney	17/1387/BR113(POW)	Cwrt-y-Gollen	SO 232 168	SS/BA
Vale of Grwyncy	17/1213/BRI28(POW)	Crug Hywel	SO 226 207	HE/IA
Vale of Grwyncy	17/3039/BRI71(POW)	Golden Grove	SO 239 178	SS/BA
Trallong	17/2150/BR043(POW)	Twyn-y-Gaer	SN 990 280	HEIIA
Trallong	17/2151/BR044(POW)	Twyn-y-Gaer	SN 970 306	HE/IA
Trallong	17/2224/BR068(POW)	Ynyshir	SN 921382	SC/BA
Trallong	17/2367/BRI03(POW)	Gam Wen	SN 934 407	RC/BA
Trallong	17/2365/BRI05(POW)	Twyn Cerrig-Cadarn	SN 948 385	RC/BA
Trallong	17/2364/BRI06(POW)	Y Crug	SN 949 379	RB/BA
Treflys	17/1871/BR066(POW)	Pen-y-Gam-Goch	SN 885 502	LCT/N
Treflys	17/2258/BR149(POW)	Banc Paderau	SN 876 525	RC/BA
Yscir	17/0739/BR042(POW)	Coed Fenn-Fach	SO 014 294	HE/IA

Yscir	17/1863/BR063(POW)	Pen-y-Crug	SO 029 303	HE/IA
Yscir	17/0214/BR138(POW)	Battle	SO 006 306	SS/BA
Yscir	17/0215/BR139(POW)	Aberyscir	SO 989 305	RC/BA
Yscir	17/3609/BR189(POW)	Fennifach	SO 017 302	SS/BA
Yscir	17/0082/BR134(POW)	Cefn Esgair	SN 974 134	RC/BA
Yscir	17/2870/BR169(POW)	Blaen-Nedd Isaf	SN 907 147	RC/BA
Yscir	17/3587/BR188(POW)	Dyffryn Nedd	SN 913 127	HE/IA

Key:

N	Neolithic	BA	Bronze Age	IA	Iron Age
LCT	Long Chambered Tomb	RC	Round or Ring Cairn	RB	Round Barrow
SS	Standing Stone	SC	Stone Circle	C	Cist
PS	Prehistoric Settlement	HE	Hill Enclosure (or hillfort)		

Note: The authors have tried to ensure the correct Welsh spellings are used for all sites that appear in this book. However, there are discrepancies with spellings of certain names. This appears to be an inherent problem, not just with SMR county lists, but also with the CADW and RCAHM(W) inventories an the Ordnance Survey. If spellings vary, then consult the NGR (National Grid Reference).

Appendix II

Tombs of the Black Mountains Group in Herefordshire and Radnorshire

Parkwood, St Margaret's, Herefordshire (1) (SO 356 335)
The precise location of this monument is unknown as it is believed to be destroyed. George Clinch remarks in 1854 that about 250 yards north-east of a medieval enclosure within St Margaret's Park Wood is a flat, horizontal slab of limestone like the upright of a 'cromlech'. He goes on to say that the stone measured approximately 9m x 3m and in places was more than 1.8m thick. In the same account, the Rev. Dr Jenkins of Hereford remarks that 'Half a century ago [1804], as stated by an old man in the neighbourhood, it [the stone slab] stood wholly free from the ground on certain upright stones. There is still at the west end of the slab, but at a slight distance from it, an upright stone, flat at the top, which may have originally been one of those on which it was supported. It seems probable that these may be the remains of a fallen cromlech.'

Visiting the site in 1921, though failing to find the monument, O.G.S. Crawford (1925:149-50) suggests it could be found on a south-west facing slope within St Margarets Wood. There is a reference to this monument in *Megalithic Enquiries* (Powell *et al.* 1969:288). At present, the whereabouts is still a mystery, although on a recent visit to the immediate area, there was a large limestone slab still visible which may represent a section of the capstone (for which see the grid reference as given above). Whether or not this represents part of the Parkwood tomb remains a question of debate.

The landscape position of the capstone is typical of others in the overall group. Parkwood would have had an almost uninterrupted view of the eastern extent of the Black Mountains and it is argued that this monument may represent the south-eastern limit of the Black Mountains Group (Children & Nash 1994:20-1). However, a probable (unexcavated) long mound (SO 440 255) is present on Garway Hill, 8km farther south. This oval-shaped mound stands around 335m OD and measures approximately 31m long by 17.5m in width, stands 2m high (at the western end) and is in a good state of preservation. The mound is orientated east-west and commands outstanding views of the eastern Black Mountains, from Dorstone Hill to Skirrid Fawr (near Abergavenny).

Long Barrow, Dunseal, Herefordshire (2) (SO 391 338)

The site remains a mystery as to its origins. The few surface finds (from ploughing) suggest a Neolithic or Early Bronze Age date. The mound itself is oval, approximately 27m x 14m in diameter and 2m high. The mound may have once been circular, therefore hinting towards a Bronze Age date. However, the authors argue that, due to its location (high on a west-facing ridge and occupying dominant views, especially to the south and west), this monument is most probably a Neolithic long barrow.

This monument along with the now destroyed Parkwood chambered tomb may mark the most southerly extent of Neolithic influence in the Golden Valley. Possibly, Dunseal Long Barrow and Parkwood represent territorial (boundary) 'markers'. Beyond these monuments, southwards, there appears to be no other monument and very little in the way of Neolithic artefacts. These monuments along with others sited around the valley peripheries could well be delineating a defined territory using tomb distribution and location. This delineation creates control and, above all, identity for the valley's inhabitants.

Cross Lodge Barrow, Dorstone, Herefordshire (3) (SO 333 417)

Three large ash trees are growing at the southern end of the mound. Possibly much larger during the Neolithic, the mound shape is of an elongated oval, approximately 18m x 10m and 2.5m high. Locally oriented (north-west/south-east) to the Golden Valley, Cross Lodge Long Barrow (as well as Arthur's Stone) embraces commanding views of the eastern ridges of the Black Mountains. During the recent past, this monument has suffered plough damage to the northern section of the mound. Indeed, a large number of stones now litter the corner of the field, some of which may belong to the original tomb structure.

During the Neolithic, Cross Lodge Long Barrow would have been visible from the valley floor and also form the large Neolithic settlement on Dorstone Hill approximately 1km north. The settlement is visible and central to both tombs, however there is no intervisibilty between the tombs.

Arthur's Stone and Cross Lodge Long Barrow are constructed in different ways, which suggests that they either date to different times and/or that they represent two different meanings. Cross Lodge Barrow is aligned to the orientation of the valley whereas Arthur's Stone may represent a valley-end territorial marker. It is probable that Arthur's Stone predates Cross Lodge Long Barrow by a considerable amount of time; probably due to the large quantities of Mesolithic flint found around and underneath Arthur's Stone.

Arthur's Stone, Dorstone, Herefordshire (4) (SO 318 431)

Arthur's Stone dates from about 3500 BC and is one of the most northerly chambered tombs of the Cotswold-Severn Group. It is one of five identifiable Neolithic monuments that dominate the Neolithic landscape of the northern reaches of the Golden Valley. Set in an oval mound (originally 26m x 17m), the tomb has nine upright stones (forming a polygonal chamber), an unorthodox right-angled passage and an enormous capstone, estimated to weigh over 25 tonnes. To the south of the capstone and chamber is a large upright sandstone slab which allegedly has a series of cupmarks on the inner face. Also present and extremely visible on the upper part of the stone is a series of dateable graffiti with a clear date of 1912. Lying directly in front of the stone and in front of the chamber, is a further single stone. O.G.S. Crawford has suggested this is actually fallen (1925), but it is more likely that, along with the upright, it forms part of a southern axis chamber.

The Woolhope Club visiting the site in July 1872 remarked that a series of stones laid out in a circular fashion surrounded the monument. It could be suggested that these may represent the outer kerbing; what is termed by the antiquarians of the day as a 'peristalith' enclosing the mound. However, an alternative view suggests that Arthur's Stone may have been trapezoidal in shape and that may have extended across the road and the northern passage placed on the side of the monument (Nash 2001). In support of this, it seems unlikely that Arthur's Stone is the only distinct oval mound within this group.

The capstone (5.8m x 3m) is split into three pieces and is oriented north-east/south-west with the south-western end pointing towards the southern section of the Golden Valley. A large section of the capstone has also split horizontally with an enormous flake collapsing into the central chamber. The capstone and uprights are made from local sandstone. The chamber has, at its western end, a false portal stone (partly blocking the doorway to the main chamber) and a passage that is oriented north. However, the passage changes direction to the north-west, pointing towards the impressive Hay Bluff (the northern extent of the Black Mountains). Crawford (1925:147) suggests the chambers of Arthur's Stone and Gwernvale are similar, although the former is much larger. The unorthodox redirection of the passage and the orientation of the capstone might suggest that Arthur's Stone was positioned deliberately so to completely encompass the whole aspect of the Black Mountains. The tomb also incorporates views from both the southern and northern extents of the Golden Valley. Indeed, many other tombs sited in the upper Wye and Usk appear to be positioned in a similar way.

Arthur's Stone along with other tombs in the area represent a continuous presence of human activity since at least the Late Mesolithic (6000-3500 BC), Mesolithic flint having been found beneath and around Arthur's Stone.

Bach Long Barrow, Bach, Herefordshire (5) (SO 277 429)

This Neolithic Long Barrow is badly damaged at the northern end. Drystone walling can be clearly seen on the woodland side of the mound. The mound is oval-shaped, approximately 13m x 10m, and 2m high.

This monument is the most north-westerly of the Golden Valley Group and is sited on a north-facing slope, overlooking the upper reaches of the Wye Valley. Its position suggests, therefore, that it may not be associated with any of the Golden Valley tombs, but, with its localised orientation (east/west) is perhaps associated with nearby Clyro Court Farm Long Barrow (212 341) and the now damaged Clyro Long Barrow (212 437), both located in Radnorshire. All three tombs would have had dominant views over the upper Wye Valley and all would have been intervisible. Unfortunately, to the north of Bach Long Barrow is dense woodland and, therefore, visibility to other monuments is difficult to ascertain.

Clyro Court Farm Long Barrow, Radnorshire (6) (SO 212 431)

The visible remains are restricted to a low mound and a few uprights., the latter delineating the remains of a small chamber and passage. The tomb has outstanding views across the upper Wye Valley and incorporates the north-western extent of the Black Mountains. In addition, Mynydd Troed, an isolated peak can also be seen, approximately 15km SSW.

This monument is valley oriented, that is, the mound shape follows the direction of the valley (south-west/north-east). Close by, and now destroyed, another long barrow existed—Clyro Long Barrow, mentioned in *Megalithic Enquiries* (1969). It is possible that this tomb may have functioned quite differently from that of the Court Farm monument, in a similar way to Arthur's Stone and Cross Lodge Barrow at Dorstone. In both cases there is no intervisibility—the Clyro Court Farm monument is positioned so that nearby Penywyrlod (3.5km) and Little Lodge Barrow (4.6km) are completely hidden from view, but at the same time having outstanding views right across the south-western flanks of the upper Wye Valley.

BIBLIOGRAPHY

Abbreviations
TWNFC - Transactions of the Woolhope Naturalists' Field Club
Arch. Camb. - Archaeologia Cambrensis

ALCOCK, L. (1965) 'Hillforts in Wales and the Marches', *Antiquity*, 39, 184-95.
ARCHAEOLOGIA CAMBRENSIS 1854, Notes by George Clinch, 148.
ATKINSON, A.J. (1972) 'Burial and Population in the British Bronze Age', in
    Lynch, F., Burgess, C. (eds.) *Prehistoric Man in Wales and the West;*
    Essays in honour of Lily F. Chitty, Bath, 107-116.
BARBER, C. & WILLIAMS, G.W. (1989) *The Ancient Stones of Wales*,
    Abergavenny, Blorenge Books.
BARKER, C.T. (1992) The Chambered Tombs of South-West Wales: A
    re-assessment of the Neolithic burial monuments of Carmarthenshire and
    Pembrokeshire, Oxbow Monograph 14.
BENDER, B. (1978) 'Gatherer-hunter to farmer: a social perspective', *World*
    Archaeology, 10, 204-422.
BOURDIEU, P. (1990) *Outline of a Theory of Practice*, CUP, Cambridge.
BRADLEY, R. (1984) 'Studying Monuments' in R. Bradley and J. Gardiner
    (eds.) Neolithic Studies: A Review of some Current Research. B.A.R.
    British Series 133. 61-66.
BREUIL, ABBÉ (1935) *Les peintures rupestres schematiques de la Peninsule*
    Iberique, Madrid.
BRITNELL, W. (1979) 'The Gwernvale Long Cairn', *Antiquity*, 53, 132-4.
BRITNELL, W. & SAVORY, H. (1984) Gwernvale and Penywyrlod: Two
    Neolithic Long Cairns in the Black Mountains of Breconshire, Cambrian
    Archaeological Monographs No.2, Cardiff.
BURNHAM, H. (1995) *A Guide to Ancient and Historic Wales*, HMSO/Cadw.
CAMPBELL, J.B. (1977) *The Upper Palaeolithic of Britain*, Croom Helm.
CASELDINE, A. (1990) *Environmental Archaeology in Wales*, Cadw Welsh
    Historical Monuments & Dept. of Archaeology, St David's University
    College, Lampeter.
CASTLEDEN, R. (1992) *Neolithic Britain: New Stone Age Sites of England,*
    Scotland and Wales, London. Routledge.
CHAPMAN, J. (1997) 'Places as Timemarks - The Social Construction of
    Prehistoric Landscapes in Eastern Hungary' in G.H.Nash (ed.) *Semiotics*
    of Landscape: Archaeology of Mind, Oxford BAR International Series
    661, 31-45.
CHILDREN, G. & NASH, G.H. (1994) Monuments in the Landscape: *The*
    Prehistoric Sites of Herefordshire, Vol. I Logaston Press, Hereford.
    (1996) Monuments in the Landscape: *The Prehistoric Sites of*
        Monmouthshire ,Vol. IV. Logaston Press, Hereford.
    (1997) Monuments in the Landscape: *The Neolithic Sites of*
        Cardiganshire, Carmarthenshire and Pembrokeshire, Vol. VII.
        Logaston Press, Hereford.
CLOUTMAN, E. (1983) Studies of the vegetational history of the Black
    Mountain Range, South Wales, Unpublished Ph.D. thesis. University of
    Wales.

CORCORAN, J. X.W.P. (1969) 'The Cotswold-Severn Group' in Powell, T.G.E., Corcoran, J.X.W.P., Lynch, F. and Scott, J.G. *Megalthic Enquiries in the West of Britain*, Liverpool University Press, Liverpool.

CRAMPTON, C.B.. & WEBLEY, D.P. (1966) ***

CRAWFORD, O.G.S. (1925) *The Long Barrows of the Cotswolds*, Gloucester.

CUNLIFFE, B. (1978) *Iron Age Communities in Britain*, Routledge & Keegan Paul, London.

DANIEL, G. (1950) *The Prehistoric Chambered Tombs of England andWales*, Cambridge, CUP, Cambridge.

DORLING, P. (1996) 'Prehistoric Monuments: A Field Guide' in D. Brinn *Prehistoric Peoples: their life and legacy*, Brecon Beacons National Park Service Publications.

DUNNING, G.C. (1943) 'A stone circle and cairn on Mynydd Epynt, Breconshire' in *Arch. Camb.* 97, 167-94.

FENTON, S.P. (1804) *Tours of Wales*, 25-26.

FOWLER, P. (1983) *Prehistoric Farming*, CUP, Cambridge.

FRAMPTON, K. (1992) *Modern Architecture: A Critical History*, Thames and Hudson, London, 57-63.

FRIED, M. (1975) *The Notion of Tribe*, Menlo Park, Calif., Cummings Publishing Co.

GAVIN ROBINSON, R.S. (1934) 'Flint workers and flint users of the Golden Valley'. *TWNFC*, 54-63.

GIBSON, A. (1986) *Neolithic and Early Bronze Age Pottery*, Shire Publications No.43.

GRØNNOW, B. (1987) 'Meiendorf and Stellmoor Revisited: An analysis of late Palaeolithic Reindeer exploration', *Acta Archaeologica*, 131-166.

GRIMES, W.F. (1932) 'Prehistoric Archaeology in Wales since 1925. The Neolithic Period', *Proceedings of the Prehistoric Society of East Anglia*, 7, 85-92.

(1936a) 'The Megalithic Monuments of Wales', *Proceedings of the Prehistoric Society*, 2, 106-139.

(1936b) 'The Long Cairns of Breconshire Black Mountains', *Archaeologia Cambrensis*, 259-282.

(1939) 'The excavation of Ty Isaf Long Cairn, Breconshireshire', *Proceedings of the Prehistoric Society*, V, 119-42.

(1951) *The Prehistory of Wales*, Cardiff, National Museum Collections.

GRINSELL, L. (1981) *Arch. Camb.*, 131-139.

HARDING, D. W. (1974) *The Iron Age in Lowland Britain*, Routledge and Kegan Paul, London.

HASELGROVE, C. (1986) 'Central Places in British Iron Age Studies', in E. Grant (ed.) *Central Places, Archaeology and History*, University of Sheffield, Sheffield.

HEALEY, E, & GREEN, S. (1984) 'The Lithic Industries' in W. Britnell & H. Savory: *Gwernvale and Penywyrlod: Two Neolithic Long Cairns in the Black Mountains of Breconshire*, Cambrian Archaeological Monographs No.2 Cardiff.

HEMP, W.J. (1935) 'Arthur's Stone, Dorstone, Herefordshire', *Archaeologia Cambrensis*, XC, 288-92.

HODDER, I. (1990) *The Domestication of Europe*, Blackwell Press, Oxford.

HOGG, A.H.A. (1975) *Hillforts of Britan*, London, Hart-Davis, MacGibbon, 57.

HOULDER, C. H. (1978) *Wales: An Archaeological Guide*, Faber & Faber, London.

HUNTLEY, B. (1990) 'European vegetation history: Palaeovegetation maps from pollen data - 13,000 yrs. B.P. to present', *Journal of Quaternary Science*, Vol.5, No. 2, 183-222, Willey.

JACOBI, R. (1980) 'The Upper Palaeolithic in Britain, with special reference to Wales', in J.A. Taylor (ed.) *Culture, Environment in Prehistoric Wales*, BAR 76, Oxford. 15-99.

JENKS, C (ed.). (1969) *Meaning and Architecture*, Design Year Book Ltd.

JONES, T. (1809)*History of the County of Brecknock,* Vol. 2.

JONES, R., BENSON-EVANS, K. & CHAMBERS, F.M. (1985) 'Human Influence upon Sedimentation in Llangorse Lake, Wales' in *Earth Surface Proceedings of Landforms*, 10, 227-235.

KINNES, I. (1992) *Non-Megalithic Long Barrows and Allied Structures in the British Neolithic*, British Museum Occasional Paper No.52, London.

LOWE, J. & WALKER, M.C. (1984) *Reconstructing Quaternary Environments*, Longmans Press, London.

MOORE, ET AL. (1984) 'The Vegetation and Development of Blanket Mires' in Moore, P.D. (ed.) *European Mires*, Academic Press, London, 203-236.

MYTUM, H. (1988) 'On-site and Off-site Evidence for Changes in Subsistence Economy: Iron Age and Romano-British West Wales' in Bintliff, J., Davidson, D. and Grant, E. (eds.) *Conceptual Issues in Environmental Archaeology*, Edinburgh University Press, 72-81.

NASH, G.H. (1997) 'Monumentality and the Landscape: The Possible Symbolic and Political Distribution of Long Chambered Tombs around the Black Mountains, Central Wales' in G.H. Nash (ed.) *Semiotics of Landscape: Archaeology of Mind*, Oxford BAR International Series 661, 17-30.

(1998) *Exchange, Status and Mobility: Mesolithic portable art of Southern Sandinavia*, Oxford BAR International Series, S710

PARKER-PEARSON, M. (1993) *Bronze Age Britain*, English Heritage.

POWELL, T.G.E., CORCORAN, J.X.W.P., LYNCH, F. & SCOTT, J.G. (1969) *Megalithic Enquiries in the West of Britain*, Liverpool University Press, Liverpool.

PRINGLE, J. & NEVILLE GEORGE, T. (1970) *British Regional Geology: South Wales*, HMSO (2nd Edition).

RCAHM(W) (1986) *An Inventory of the Ancient Monuments in Breconshire (Brycheiniog): Later Prehistoric Monuments and Unenclosed Settlements to 1000 A.D*, (Part I). HMSO.

RCAHM(W) (1997) *An Inventory of the Ancient Monuments in Breconshire (Brycheiniog): The Prehistoric and Roman Monuments*, (Part II). HMSO.

RENFREW, C. (1979) *Investigations in Orkney*, London, Society of Antiquaries.

SAVORY, H.N. (1980a) Guide Catalogue of the Bronze Age Collections, National Museum of Wales, Cardiff.

(1980b) 'The Neolithic in Wales', in J.A.Taylor (ed.) *Culture and Environment in Prehistoric Wales*, British Archaeological Report No.76, Oxford. 207-232.

SMITH, C. (1992) *Late stone Age Hunters of the British Isles*, Routledge, London.

SMITH, A.G. & CLOUTMAN, E. (1988) 'Reconstruction of Holocene vegetation history in three dimensions at Waun-Fignen-Felen, an upland site in South Wales, *Phil. Transactions. of Royal. Society*, London, B 322, 159-219.

SMITH, R.T. & TAYLOR, J.A. (1969) 'The post-glacial development of Vegetarian soils in Northern Carmarthenshire' in *Transactions of the Institute of British Geogrpahy*, 48, 77-95.

STANFORD, S.C. (1974) *Croft Ambrey: Excavations carried out for the Woolhope Naturalists' Field Club*
(1991) *The Archaeology of The Welsh Marches* (2nd Ed.), S.C. Stanford, 2-73.

STARTIN, B. & BRADLEY, R. (1981) 'Some notes on work organisation and society in Prehistoric Wessex' in Ruggles, C.N.L. & Whittle, A.W.R. (eds.) *Astronomy and Society in Britan during the period 4000-1500BC*, BAR Oxford, 289-96.

STUIVER, M., REIMER, P.J., BARD, E., BECK, J.W., BURR, G.S., HUGHEN, K.A., KROMER, B., McCORMAC, F.G., v.d.PLICHT, J. and SPURK, M. (1998) 'Marine delta 14C and radiocarbon ages' in *Radiocarbon*, University of Edinburgh Press.

TAYLOR, J.A. (ed.) (1980) *Prehistoric Wales*, BAR Oxford Report No.76.

THOM, A. (1967) *Megalithic Sites in Britain*, London, OP.

THOMAS, K.W. (1965) 'The Stratigraphy and pollen analysis of a raised peat bog at Llanllwch, near Carmarthen', *New Phytol*, 64, 101-117.

TILLEY, C. (1994) *A Phenomenology of Landscape: Places, Paths and Monuments*, Berg, Oxford.

TRIGGER, B. (1982) *Ethnography by Archaeologists: 1978*, Procceedings of the American Ethnological Society.

TURNER, J. (1964) 'The anthropogenic factor in vegetational history 1: Tregaron and Whixall mosses', *New Phytol*, 63, 73-89.

VULLIAMY, C.E. (1921) 'The Excavation of a Megalithic Tomb in Breconshire', *Archaeologia Cambrensis*, 7th ser. (LXXVI), 300-5.
(1923) 'Further excavations in the Long Barrows at Ffostyll', *Archaeologia Cambrensis*, 7th ser. iii (LXXVIII), 320-4.
(1929) 'Excavation of an unrecorded Long Barrow in Wales', *Man*, XXIX, No.29, 34-6.

WILLIAMS, A.H. (1941) *An Introduction to the History of Wales*, Vol 1, University of Wales Press, Cardiff.

WIMBLE, G. (1986) 'Pollen' in Warrilow, W., Owen, G. and Brittnell, W.J. 1986 Proceedings of the Prehistoric Society 52, Microfiche 5-9.

WILTSHIRE, P.E.J. & MOORE, P.D. (1983) Palaeovegetation and palaeo-hydrology in upland Britain, in Gergory K.J. (ed.) *Background to Palaeohydrology*, John Wiley & Sons, London, 433-451.

WYMER, J.J. (1977) *Gazetteer of Mesolithic sites in England and Wales*, C.B.A. (Council for British Archaeology), Research Report No.22.

YESNER, D.R. (1980) 'Marine Hunter-Gatherers - Ecology and Prehistory', *Current Anthropology*, 21, 727-750.